AF130761

MIX
Papier aus verantwortungsvollen Quellen
Paper from responsible sources
FSC® C105338

Irini Varvouzou

Capital Market Anomalies

Explained by human´s irrationality

Anchor Academic
Publishing

Varvouzou, Irini: Capital Market Anomalies: Explained by human´s irrationality, Hamburg, Diplomica Verlag GmbH 2012

ISBN: 978-3-95489-030-9
Print: Anchor Academic Publishing, an Imprint of Diplomica® Verlag GmbH, Hamburg, 2012

Bibliographical Information of the German National Library:
The German National Library lists this publication in the German National Bibliography. Detailed bibliographic data can be found at: http://dnb.d-nb.de

The digital publication (eBook) of this work with the ISBN 978-3-95489-530-4 can be purchased on the general market or directly from the publisher.

All rights reserved. This publication may not be reproduced, stored in a retrieval system or transmitted, in any form or by any means, electronic, mechanical, photocopying, recording or otherwise, without the prior permission of the publishers.

Dieses Werk ist urheberrechtlich geschützt. Die dadurch begründeten Rechte, insbesondere die der Übersetzung, des Nachdrucks, des Vortrags, der Entnahme von Abbildungen und Tabellen, der Funksendung, der Mikroverfilmung oder der Vervielfältigung auf anderen Wegen und der Speicherung in Datenverarbeitungsanlagen, bleiben, auch bei nur auszugsweiser Verwertung, vorbehalten. Eine Vervielfältigung dieses Werkes oder von Teilen dieses Werkes ist auch im Einzelfall nur in den Grenzen der gesetzlichen Bestimmungen des Urheberrechtsgesetzes der Bundesrepublik Deutschland in der jeweils geltenden Fassung zulässig. Sie ist grundsätzlich vergütungspflichtig. Zuwiderhandlungen unterliegen den Strafbestimmungen des Urheberrechtes.

Die Wiedergabe von Gebrauchsnamen, Handelsnamen, Warenbezeichnungen usw. in diesem Werk berechtigt auch ohne besondere Kennzeichnung nicht zu der Annahme, dass solche Namen im Sinne der Warenzeichen- und Markenschutz-Gesetzgebung als frei zu betrachten wären und daher von jedermann benutzt werden dürften.

Die Informationen in diesem Werk wurden mit Sorgfalt erarbeitet. Dennoch können Fehler nicht vollständig ausgeschlossen werden, und der Diplomica Verlag, die Autoren oder Übersetzer übernehmen keine juristische Verantwortung oder irgendeine Haftung für evtl. verbliebene fehlerhafte Angaben und deren Folgen.

© Anchor Academic Publishing ein Imprint der Diplomica® Verlag GmbH
http://www.diplomica-verlag.de, Hamburg 2012
Printed in Germany

Table of Contents

1. Introduction

1.1. Problem Specification

Why do small caps achieve higher risk-adjusted yields than large caps ? Why do stock prices increase or decrease upon an index entry respectively deletion ? Why does January records higher yields than the remaining months of the year ? These as well as other observed capital market anomalies respectively phenomena could insufficiently be explained by the classical capital market theory, which proceeds on the assumption, that all correspondent information are reflected in the stock prices, all negative effects are directly balanced on the market level and efficiency of arbitrage principle exists as well as all market participants are acting rational, i.e. optimizing their benefits in the sense of the homo oeconomicus. This motivated some economists and psychologists to research the influences on the formation of prices on the capital market while including behavioural scientific findings. Hence in 1980s Behavioural Finance has been developed, which challenges the homo oeconomicus and came to the conclusion, that humans are not only acting rational, but that they are influenced by emotions, knowledge as well as experiences, i.e. are irrational. Thus this new scientific behavioural oriented theory, which is today a separate branch of research, contradicts the classical capital market theory and supplies explanations for the observed phenomena on the capital market.

1.2. Objective

The aim of this thesis is to demonstrate how human behaviour influences the development on the capital market respectively Behavioural Finance serves as explanation for the empirically observed capital market anomalies.

1.3. Structure

This thesis begins with the introduction of the theoretical basis of Behavioural Finance respectively its emergence, tasks as well as aims will be explained in detail. Subsequently human's heuristics as well as anomalies respectively irrationalities in their decision making process will be demonstrated. In the third chapter the capital market anomalies respectively phenomena as well as their rational respectively economical reasons and irrational respectively behavioural reasons for their existence will be described. The fourth chapter covers empirical evidence for their existence as well as for the insufficient explanatory power of the classical capital market theory. Concluding a critical acclaim, target achievement as well as perspective concerning Behavioural Finance will be given.

2. Theoretical Basis of Behavioural Finance

There are many definitions explaining the term Behavioural Finance. The three most commonly known definitions are as per the economists Thaler, Shefrin and Sewell. Thaler defines Behavioural Finance as an just open minded finance whereas Shefrin describes it as a fast-growing area that concerns with the influence of psychology on the behaviour of financial investors. The last economist Sewell determines it as a study, which researches the question to which extent psychical factors influence the behaviour of the market participants and their reactions the development of the financial markets. However, all definitions express the same meaning, namely that it is a behaviour-oriented financial market theory.[1]

Behavioural Finance has been developed, due to the insufficient explanatory power and predictive efficiency of classical capital market theories concerning capital market's behaviour and its phenomena. Thus its task is to explain these capital market anomalies and its phenomena e.g. bubbles, as well as its final occurrences on the financial markets e.g. overreaction und thus the pricing and performance of stocks e.g. short terms stock volatilies and to search for reasons of market inefficiencies, while including the human behaviour, i.e. psychological and sociological aspects.[2]

Not the substitution, but a paradigm shift, i.e. the further development of the existing neoclassical capital market theory – in which all information are priced into the stock prices, error compensation on the market stage and efficiency of arbitrage principle exists as well as all market participants are acting rational, i.e. optimizing their benefits in the sense of the homo oeconomicus – is in the front of this theory respectively the development of an expectation development and information processing theory. This paradigm shift includes the replacement of the homo oeconomicus by human's bounded rationality. Thus Behavioural Finance tries to create a connection between existing economical models and the reality.[3]

The target of Behavioural Finance is to identify factors, which influence human's decision making process, which consists of three steps, namely the information perception, information processing and the decision making itself. In this way Behavioural Finance

---

[1] Cp. Häcker, J. (2009), p. 83; Thaler, R.H. (1993), p. xvii.
[2] Cp. Häcker, J. (2009), p. 82; Nolte, D. (2009), p. 105; Piwinger, M. (2009), p. 24.
[3] Cp. Decker, M. (2009), p. 7.

9

disclose a set of heuristics and systematic behavioural anomalies, which lead to faulty decisions, due to restricted information level caused by information costs, limited cognitive abilities caused by complex decisional situations and psychical stress, i.e. irrationality. This bounded rationality leads to faulty behaviour, which influences the capital market.[4]

2.1. Heuristics

As already explained in point two, in reality humans do not act in the sense of the homo oeconomicus, but are rational bounded. This rational bounded behaviour is reflected in the daily decision making process, where uncertainty exists, time, knowledge and information are limited and the complexity is high. In order to be able to make decisions under such suboptimal conditions, humans apply to heuristics.[5]

The term heuristic derives from the Greek word heurisco, which denotes to find. It is a cognitive method or strategy to solve problems, i.e. to come to decisions. Easily explained, they are mental shortcuts or rules of thumb, which facilitate and accelerate the solution of problems, i.e. the decision making process, if the above mentioned basic conditions are given.[6]

Heuristics will be applied conscious or unconscious. There is no clearly differentiation between conscious and unconscious heuristics. Conscious heuristics can become unconscious, if they will permanently be used whereas unconscious heuristics can be made aware und thus become conscious.[7]

The application of heuristics saves resources and time, which in turn will be used for other decisions. Hence they increase the efficiency of the thinking process.[8]

The results of heuristics are often correctly, but they also lead to wrong results, i.e. systematic judgemental bias, due to too strong complexity reduction and the herewith connected neglect of information.[9]

There exist three types of heuristics, which are the availability heuristic, representative heuristic and anchoring heuristic. Some authors do not classify them, but subsume them

---

[4] Cp. Fiala, J., Merten, H.-L. (2008), p. 34; Stanzel, M. (2007), p. 101.
[5] Cp. Fieseler, C., (2008); p. 117; Häcker, J. (2009), p. 87.
[6] Cp. Jedrowiak, J. (2008), p. 127; Kitzmann, A. (2009), p. 18; Rutkowski, L. (2008), p. 15; Ziegenbalg, B., Ziegenbalg, J., Ziegenbalg, O. (2007), p. 101.
[7] Cp. Noack, D. (2008), p. 18; Stanzel, M. (2007), p. 105.
[8] Cp. Greiner, M. (2008), p. 374; Gruß, C. (2008), p. 56.
[9] Cp. Unger, A., Unger, F., Raab, G. (2010), p. 129.

10

as judgmental heuristics. In contrary, others classify them as heuristics, which serve to reduce the complexity – availability heuristic – and heuristics, which serve to accelerate the decision making process – representative heuristic and anchoring heuristic – .[10] These heuristics will be explained in the following.

2.1.1. Availability Heuristic

In order to make rush decisions humans apply to the availability heuristic by estimating the occurrence probability respectively the frequency of an event. Thereby they refer to already existing information in their minds, which represent the results of their made experiences. The easier humans remember an event and the more examples are available, i.e. the ease with which they come into mind the more probable and frequent it will be estimated. This process is also known as cognitive availability, which serves to reduce complexity, which in turn involves the neglect of information, which are not easy accessible and available.[11]

This heuristic leads to the overvaluation of information, which indicate a high subjective availability ratio, i.e. updated, frequent, easy accessible, very conspicuous, illustrative and easy understandable information. This in turn results in systematic biases in the decision making, errors and cognitive deception, i.e. it influences the estimation of the occurrence probability respectively the frequency of an event and hence the decision.[12]

This will be illustrated by the research done by Tversky and Kahneman:

They read two lists to test persons. The first list covered 19 names of famous men and 20 names of less celebrated women. The second list covered 20 names of famous women and 19 names of less celebrated men. The test persons should estimate, if the lists covered more women or men. The result showed, that over 50 percent of the participants remembered better the famous names and approximately 80 percent overvalued the number of this gender, who bears the famous name, i.e. they overestimated the names of the men indicated in the first list and the names of the women indicated in the second list.[13]

---

[10] Cp. Goldberg, J., Nitzsch, R. (2004), p. 51; Holtfort, T. (2009), p. 20; Riesenhuber, M. (2006), p. 144.
[11] Cp. Lisbach, B., Zacharopoulos, M. (2007), p. 36; Raab, G., Unger, F. (2005), p. 121; Schwarz, N. (1997), p. 357; Titzkus, T. (2005), p. 87; Zuzak, M.T. (2008), p. 45.
[12] Cp. Schweiger, W. (2007), p. 144; Wunderle, S. (2006), p. 32.
[13] Cp. Raab, G., Unger, F. (2005), p. 122.

This example shows, that it is easier for humans to make decisions, based on the factor famous (easy accessible), as famous persons are often (frequent) presented on TV or magazines (updated, illustrative, easy understandable), either in a negative or positive way (very conspicuous), which in turn results in wrong estimation of the number of the genders.

2.1.2. Representative Heuristic

Representative heuristic is the second rule of thumb, which humans apply to in order to come to a rush decision. It is human's tendency to think, estimate, evaluate and judge in patterns of thinking, i.e. in schemes. More precisely, they generalize persons, objects, events or phenomena based on cursorily characteristics, experiences or observations, which they made in the past. This generalization is based on similarities, e.g. between a sample and population, an element and a category or a cause and an effect. This process is also known as inductive conclusion, which serves to accelerate the decision making process, which will be reached by this generalization.[14]

This heuristic leads to biases in probability estimations and hence overvaluation of information or events, the higher characteristics, previously made experiences and observations correspond to the actual situation, i.e. if they suit to an existing scheme respectively are typical. That in turn results to wrong decisions.[15]

This heuristic involves several expressions, which are gamblers fallacy, also known as Monte-Carlo-Effect or law of small numbers, conjunction fallacy, conditional probability fallacy and ecological fallacy. In order not to extrapolate the frame of this thesis only the first two expressions will be explained in detail. Gamblers fallacy is human's belief, that chances for something with a fixed probability increase or decrease depend on recent occurrences. Conjunction fallacy is human's tendency to breach probability axioms. More detailed, they overestimate the probability of two connected events than the probability of each individual event.[16]

Gambler's fallacy will be exemplified based on investigations done in a casino by Tversky and Kahneman: They observed roulette players and examined, if ten times black

---

[14] Cp. Goldberg, J., Nitzsch, R. (2004), p. 72; Nitzsch, R., Stolz, O. (2006), p. 158-159; Reimann, M. (2005), p.81; Riesenhuber, M. (2006), p. 89.
[15] Cp. Voigt, S. (2008), p. 28.
[16] Cp. Andrews, P.W., Haselton, M.G., Nettle, D. (2005), p. 727; Böhme, U. (2009), p. 5; Decker, M. (2009), p. 29-30; Imbacher, H., Jünemann, B. (2007), p. 46.

came up, most of the players tend to bet on the red for the eleventh drawn, as is it not typical eleven times to came up black.[17]

The investigation shows, that the probability of the first option has been overestimated whereas both options include the same probability.

The conjunction fallacy will be exemplified by their experiment, in which test persons shall make their estimations about a hypothetical person, based on the following information. The hypothetical person is a women, 31 years old, very intelligent and doesn't mince matters. She studied philosophy and during her study period she dealt with matters such as social justice and discrimination. Additionally she participated on the demonstration again the nuclear power plant. After these basic information the test persons shall estimate which of both further personal traits are more probable. The first information was, that she is a bank clerk and the second information was, that she is a bank clerk and engaged in the women movement. The result showed, that the test persons estimated the second trait as more probable as somebody who studied philosophy and dealt with social and discrimination matters must also be engaged in women movement.[18]

This example shows, that humans overestimate the probability of two connected events whereas the probability of two connected events is never higher than the probability of a single event.

2.1.3. Anchoring Heuristic

The anchoring heuristic is the last heuristic, which will be demonstrated in this thesis. Just like the representative heuristic it serves to accelerate the decision making process. This will be reached by orientation on a reference point – in this regard a so called anchor, which can be an existing information or opinion – if humans make their decisions, forecasts or estimations. This anchor will afterwards be adjusted by newly obtained information.[19]

This heuristic leads to biases in decision making, due to drag on of the anchor adjustment. This occurs as humans tend to adhere to their previous anchors, even though the new information contradicts already existing anchor. Hence they make their decisions,

---

[17] Cp. Nitzsch, R. (2006), p. 28.
[18] Cp. Crupi, V., Hartmann, S. (2010), p. 91; Weber, J. (2008), p. 224.
[19] Cp. Schmeisser, W. (2010), p. 261; Zuzak, M.T.(2008), p. 46.

forecasts and estimations close to their previous subjective anchor, which has incompletely or incorrectly been adjusted, which in turn leads to a partly or totally neglect of new information.[20]

This will be illustrated by an investigation done by Tversky and Kahneman:

Two groups of students obtained an arithmetic problem, which they should solve, i.e. estimate the solution within five seconds. The task of the first group was to provide an estimated solution for the arithmetic problem 1*2*3*4*5*6*7*8 and the second group should provide an estimated solution for the arithmetic problem 8*7*6*5*4*3*2*1. The first group estimated a result of 512 and the second group estimated a result of 2250.[21]

This example shows, that both groups used the first digit as their anchor. Hence the first group obtained a lower result than the second group. It evidences, that the final decision depends on the firstly set anchor, which in turn influences the decision.[22]

The described heuristics are explanations for the behavioural anomalies, which arise in the decision making process and which will be described in the following.

2.2. Behavioural Anomalies/Irrationalities

The human decision making process involves three stages, which are the information perception, information processing and decision making. In all of those three stages behavioural anomalies arise. These irrationalities will be described in the following.

2.2.1. Information Perception Anomalies

The information perception is the first stage of the decision making process. As humans have bounded information processing capacities, they try to filter the most important information already in this stage. Arising anomalies during the information perception are framing, risk sensitiveness, selective perception and adoption of authoritarian opinions. In order not to extrapolate the frame of this thesis, the focus will be laid only on the first three mentioned anomalies.[23]

---

[20] Cp. Breuer, W., Gürtler, M., Schuhmacher, F. (2006), p. 259; Hirsch, B.(2007), p. 252.
[21] Cp. Decker, M. (2009), p. 31.
[22] Cp. Jeske, K.-J. (2008), p 75.
[23] Cp. Schmies, C. (2007), p. 170.

2.2.1.1. Framing Effect

Framing is the way how an information, situation or choice will be presented respectively framed, e.g. orally, in written, but also the sequence of the information and the environment where the information will be perceived.[24]

This anomaly influences the perception and hence the decision, i.e. leads to the result, that the same information will be differently perceived, evaluated and thus faulty allocated.[25]

This will be illustrated with reference to the Asian disease problem investigated by Tversky and Kahneman:

Scientists were preparing for the outbreak of an Asian disease, which was expected to hit the USA. Therefore they proposed two programs to reduce the number of affected victims. If the first program is accepted, 4,000 of the captioned 10,000 people will certainly be saved. If the second program is accepted, there is a 40 percent probability, that 10,000 will be saved and a 60 percent probability, that nobody will be saved. Most of the people surveyed selected the first program. Now these two options were presented in another way. If the first program is accepted, 6,000 of the captioned 10,000 people will certainly die. If the second program is accepted, there is a 40 percent probability, that nobody will die and a 60 percent probability, that 10,000 will die. Most of the people surveyed selected the second program.[26]

Whereby both presentations lead to the same result, most of the surveyed choose the first alternative in the first presentation, named winner's perspective or survival frame and the second alternative in the second presentation, named loss perspective or mortality frame. The most overvalued secure values in the first presentation in a positive way, i.e. to safe life and in the second presentation in a negative way, i.e. to kill life. It also implies, that the most act risk avers in the first presentation and risk seeking in the second presentation.

2.2.1.2. Risk Sensitiveness

Risk sensitiveness is human's perception of dangers and evaluation of the risks or consequences involved, which are affected by human's subjective understanding of the

---

[24] Cp. Wahren, H.-K. (2009), p. 72.
[25] Cp. Schmies, C. (2007), p. 170.
[26] Cp. Grauwe, P., Grimaldi, M. (2006), p. 12; Kahneman, D., Tversky, A. (1981), p. 453-458, Steul, M. (2003), p. 70.

term risk. Human's risk sensitiveness depends on quantitative (objective) and qualitative (subjective) factors, which lead to different perception and evaluation of risks and hence faulty decisions.[27]

Quantitative factors are the probability or the relative frequency of the risk occurrence and the amount or extend of damage. Risks, which are faced more often will be undervalued, e.g. car accidents whereas those, who are rarely faced, will be overvalued, e.g. accidents during go by train. The same phenomenon applies also to risks, which amount or extend of damage is high, e.g. flying. These risks will be overvalued whereas those with a minor damage, e.g. driving, will be undervalued.[28]

Qualitative factors are the characteristics of the risk source, the risk consequence and individuals. Characteristics of the risk source involve the geographical distance and the accountability and responsibility of the risk source. Risks, which are close to the risk source, e.g. handy radiation caused by a transmission mast, will be overvalued whereas those whose distance is bigger, will be undervalued. The same overvaluation occurs, if risks will be attributed to humans, e.g. Chernobyl whereas those who will be assigned to nature, e.g. natural disaster, will be undervalued.[29]

Characteristics of the risk consequence involve the below explained points:[30]

Congruity of risk and benefit allocation: Risks will be undervalued, if the benefits arise immediately, e.g. smoking whereas risks, whose benefits concern others, arise with time lag or are not traceable, will be overvalued, e.g. passive smoking.

Irreversibility of risk consequences: Risk consequences, which are reversible, e.g. property damages, will be undervalued whereas irreversible risk consequences, e.g. radiation contaminated people caused by a power plant explosion, will be overvalued.

Controllability of risks: Risks, which can be controlled, e.g. driving, will be undervalued as humans tend to overvalue their abilities especially of everyday usually practices. In contrast, uncontrollable risks, e.g. flying, epidemic plagues and nuclear waste, will be overvalued as humans have the feeling to be unable to control something whenever they rely on other humans or techniques.

---

[27] Cp. Strohmeier, G. (2007), p. 32.

[28] Cp. Petermann, T., Revermann, C., Scherz, C. (2006), p. 140.

[29] Cp. Grunenberg, H, Heinrichs, H. (2009), p. 33; Günther, A., Haubl, R., Meyer, P., Stengel, M., Wüstner, K. (1998), p. 168; Wiedemann, P. (2010), p. 103.

[30] Cp. Anwander Phan-huy, S. (1998), p. 10; Bogun,, R. (2008), p. 129; Brandl, P.K. (2010), p. 88-89; Brühwiler, B. (1994), p. 70; König, W. (2010), p. 217; Mehl, F. (2001), p. 240; Schütz, H., Wiedemann, P.M. (2005), p. 80.

Personal involvement: Risks will be overvalued, if someone directly or its environment is concerned with it. An investigation shows, that people, who become redundant or suffer a disease estimate the risk to become redundant and ill again higher than those who haven't made experiences with unemployment or a disease.

Voluntariness of risk taking: Voluntary taken risks, e.g. smoking and driving, will be undervalued and much more accepted than risks, which will be involuntary taken, i.e. external imposed risks, like nuclear power plant and irradiation of food.

Risk awareness level: Risks, which will be daily faced and are well known, e.g. on the workplace, will be undervalued than those who are new und unknown.

Time delayed risk effects: Risks, whose effects occur with a time delay, like cancer by smokers, are subject to lower risk sensitiveness than those, whose consequences arise directly, e.g. death by car accident.

Individual-related characteristics involve human's risk propensity. Risk seeking humans undervalue risks whereas risk averse humans overvalue them. Last individual-related traits are socio-demographic factors like the age. Young people indicate higher risk sensitiveness than old people.[31]

Aside of framing the risk sensitiveness will additionally be influenced by control illusion and optimism.[32]

This anomaly is linked to the next explained anomaly, named selective perception.[33]

2.2.1.3. Selective Perception

Selective perception is human's tendency to notice, filter and perceive only information, which corresponds to their own conceptions, hypotheses, actions and opinions. Contrary information will be eliminated, ignored or neglected. The reason for this behaviour is the cognitive dissonance. More in detail, humans seek for consistency and thus try to avoid the internal conflict, which arises, if they notice, that their conceptions, hypotheses, actions and opinions are inconsistent. Easily explained, it is a justification process,

---

[31] Cp. Müller-Reichart, M. (1994), p. 67-81; Wahren, H.-K. (2009), p. 99.
[32] Cp. Bergold, U., Mayer, B. (2005), p. 26; Schmidt, K. (2009), p. 541.
[33] Cp. Müller-Reichart, M. (1994), p. 89.

which makes the misfit fit, in order to avoid the psychological pain. Hence selective perception serves as a protective shield for human's psyche.[34]

This anomaly leads to an alleviated perception, due to which only information in context to the conceptions, hypotheses, actions and opinions are accepted while contradictory information are ignored. It also leads to confirmation bias, due to the unconsciously searching of information, which confirm the conceptions, hypotheses, actions and opinions. Moreover it results in selective bias, were contradictory information will be interpreted in a way, that they conform to the initial conceptions, hypotheses, actions and opinions. Also it leads to overhasty decisions, in order to avoid a justification pressure. Finally, it involves the adherence of prejudices too.[35]

This will be illustrated by the following example:

A smoker developed health problems, due to which his doctor advised him to stop smoking and handed out an information brochure for a rehabilitation to support his recovery. Upon reading the information, that smoking causes cancer the internal conflict arose, which he reduced by neglecting the information, that it causes cancer. Additionally he achieved internal harmony by searching for supporting information, which proved that he is right. In this case he stated, that his grandpa is a smoker aged 90 years and in good health. Another way is that he said, that smoking provides relaxation and that positive effects like that cannot promote health problems or cause cancer. Another method to which he applied to, was to tell, that cancer will only arise, when smoking too much.[36]

This example shows, that the smoker neglects, ignores and eliminates contradictory information, which in turn leads to biases in its risk perception.

2.2.2. Information Processing Anomalies

The information processing is the penultimate step of the decision making process. Affiliated irrational processes during the information perception are the reference point effect, mental accounting and loss aversion.

---

[34] Cp. Behrens, B. (2010), p. 78; Goldberg, J., Nitzsch, R. (2004), p. 210-211; Hermann, A. (2007), p. 166; Hofmann-Unger, K., Unger, C. (2007), p. 144; Michelis, D. (2009), p. 76; Schön, M. (2006), p. 42; Stanzel, M. (2007), p. 107.

[35] Cp. Egloff, B. (2002), p. 57; Jost, P-.J. (2008), p. 307; Junge, P. (2010), p. 118; Kottke, N. (2005), p. 66; Lehment, T., Krumbach-Mollenhauer, P. (2007), p. 82; Mieth, D. (2004), p. 91; Romppel, A. (2006), p. 239; Völker, R. (2008), p. 96.

[36] Cp. Hausmann, C. (2009), p. 91-92; Hornung, R., Lächler, J. (2006), p. 104-105; Schön, M. (2006), p. 18.

2.2.2.1. Reference Point Effect

As already explained in 2.1.3., humans are geared to a subjective reference point respectively anchor. This reference point represents a part also in the information processing. In this sense the reference point is human's subjective expectation. Consequences of an alternative, e.g. gains or losses will be not evaluated absolutely, but relatively to this reference point. More detailed, deviations close to the reference point will be evaluated higher than deviations, which are far apart from it.[37]

This result in the fact, that the same consequences, e.g. gains or losses will be differently evaluated, based on the distance to the individual set reference point, i.e. the difference between the actual situation and the expectation.[38]

This will be clarified by the following example:

Two women are visited a museum on a National Holiday. When woman A arrived at the museum she was told, that due to National Holiday the entrance fee is 6 Euro instead of the regular 10 Euro. Women B assumed, that due to the National Holiday the entrance would be for free. When she arrived at the museum she was told, that the entrance fee is 6 Euro. Whereas both cost situations are identical, women A sensed the price deduction as a gain of 4 Euro and women B as a loss of 6 Euro.[39]

This example shows, that the subjective reference point of both women – woman A 10 Euro and woman B 0 Euro – influences, if a consequence will be considered as a gain or a loss.

The reference point effect serves as basis to the following described anomalies, which are mental accounting and loss aversion.

2.2.2.2. Mental Accounting

Mental accounting is a complex reducing mental process, which involves the categorization, codification and evaluation of alternatives respectively its consequences, as well as the way how they will be segregated or integrated. Easily explained, humans divide alternatives e.g. expenditures, incomes, months, and allocate them to different, not connected mental accounts, based on which they make their decisions. Each mental account involves a subjective reference point, as well as a cost and benefit side respectively loss

---

[37] Cp. Haas, A., Scheufele, B. (2008), p. 57; Wunderle, S. (2006), p. 43; Zayer, E. (2007), p. 67.
[38] Cp. Diller, H. (2008), p. 141; Greiner, M. (2008), p. 376.
[39] Cp. Lupert, P. (2010), p. 29.

and gain side. This mental process can be compared to the accounting of a company whereas companies create them according to the accounting rules. The way human's create their mental accounts and segregate or integrate its sides is constituted by hedonic editing. Simplified said, it will be done in a way where they reach the most satisfaction, feel more convenient, maximize their benefits and is more attractive, i.e. avoids losses and cognitive dissonance.[40]

Mental accounting leads to different evaluations and thus suboptimal decisions, as consequences of an alternative will not be evaluated as a whole, but concentrated only on one account. Thereby dependences and interdependences to other mental accounts will be neglected.[41]

This will be exemplified by the research of Tversky and Kahneman:

They confronted test persons with the following situations. In the first situation they intended to visit a theatre for which they had to purchase an entrance card for 10 dollar. When arriving at the theatre they noticed that they lost 10 dollar. Would they spend another 10 dollar to visit the theatre? In the second situation they already bought the entrance card for 10 dollar beforehand. When arriving at the theatre they noticed that they lost the entrance card. Would they spend another 10 dollar to visit the theatre? The result of the survey was that in the first situation 88 percent of the test persons would spend another 10 dollar to visit the theatre whereas in the second situation only 46 percent were willing to spend further 10 dollar.[42]

Whereas the objective amount, which has to be spend in both situations – 20 dollar – is identical, it results in different subjective evaluations and decisions. More precisely, in the first situation two mental accounts have been created – one, which is classified as entertainment and one, which is classified as bad luck – , i.e. segregation of consequences. Hence the loss of money has been booked on the mental account bad luck whereas the mental account for entertainment hasn't been charged. Therefore the expense of further 10 dollar would charge the mental account entertainment only ones. Thus the subjective value of the card amounts to 10 dollar. In the second situation only one mental account – entertainment – has been created, i.e. integration of consequences. Hence the loss of the entrance card has been booked on this one account. Therefore a

[40] Cp. Kottke, N. (2005), p. 97; Nolte, D. (2009), p. 112.
[41] Cp. Schmeisser, W. (2001), p. 261; Werner, C. (2009), p. 26.
[42] Cp. Kahneman, D., Tversky, A. (1981), p. 453-458.

further expense of 10 dollar would charge this account twice. Thus the subjective value amounts to 20 dollar.

This anomaly has an impact on the next anomaly, named loss aversion.[43]

2.2.2.3. Loss Aversion

Loss aversion is human's tendency to evaluate consequences, e.g. gains and losses, of the same amount, differently. Thereby they refer to a subjective set reference point. Contrary to the reference point effect, the evaluation of changes do not depend on the deviation to the reference point, but the same deviation will be differently evaluated, namely realized losses will be perceived higher than realized gains in the same extend.[44] Loss aversion leads to the endowment effect, status quo bias and disposition effect. The endowment effect is the phenomenon that humans place a higher value on something they possess relative to something they do not. More precisely, they demand a higher price for an item they own than they would be prepared to pay for it. This in turn induces humans to stick to status quo, which is human's tendency to avoid changes and hence to remain at status quo as the reward for giving up the property will be evaluated lower as the value they would receive in return. This again is connected with the disposition effect, while losses will be sit out whereas gains will be realized to fast.[45]

This will be illustrated by the investigation of Thaler, Kahneman and Knetsch:

A group of students were divided into two groups - sellers and buyers. The sellers obtained a coffee cup and should inform at which price they would be ready to sell the cup. The buyers should decide at which price they would be ready to acquire the cup. The prices ranging from 0.50 Euro to 9.50 Euro. The sellers decided to sell the cup at a price of 7.12 Euro whereas the buyers were ready to purchase the cup at a price of 3.12 Euro.[46]

This example shows, that the sellers mentioned a higher sales price than the buyers. Additionally, whereas both situations implicate the same changes in seller's total assets, they decided no to sell the cup, but to keep it in their property and to remain at status quo, i.e. they preferred avoiding losses than acquiring gains.

---

[43] Cp. Nitzsch, R. (2006), p. 105.
[44] Cp. Drabe, K., Kondert, K., Lippert, T., Neusel, T., Schirp, W. (2009), p. 104;. Gürtler, M. Hartmann, N. (2005), p. 373; Lindenmeier, J., Tscheulin, D.K. (2009), p. 13.
[45] Cp. Faith, C.M. (2007), p. 49; Heun, M. (2007), p. 60; Kiser, R. (2010), p. 122; Tiggelaar, B. (2010), p. 36.
[46] Cp. Felser, G. (2010), p. 198; Langer, T. (1999), p. 20.

Also this anomaly will be influenced by the information perception anomaly framing.[47] This irrationality has an impact on the decision making anomalies, named cognitive dissonance and regret avoidance, which will be described in the following.[48]

2.2.3. Decision Making Anomalies

The last step of the human decision making process is the decision making itself. Related anomalies in this step are the cognitive dissonance, regret avoidance and overconfidence.

2.2.3.1. Cognitive Dissonance

This anomaly has already been touched on within the scope of the information perception anomalies. In this sense, cognitive dissonance arises, if humans have to make decisions respectively have to choose between two or more alternatives. The selected alternative bears consequences. These consequences are the advantages of the rejected alternative, which in return are the disadvantages of the selected alternative. An alternative respectively decision, which has subsequently been proved as faulty place humans under pressure to justify and thus an internal conflict respectively cognitive dissonance arises. As already mentioned, humans seek for internal harmony, which will be reached by the reduction of this emotional condition. [49]

The reduction of this anomaly leads to selective decision bias. More precisely, further made decisions orient on the previous one in order to prove and justify its accuracy. Hence the previously made decision will be not revised, which in turn leads to further faulty decisions. It also results in confirmation bias, which involves the consciously seek of information, which confirm and support the selected alternative. At the same time contradictory information will be rejected. The spreading apart effect, which is the upgrading of the selected alternative and devaluation of the rejected alternative is a further bias, which arises during this justification process. Latter involving effect is the disposition effect, i.e. humans tendency to rather realize gains than losses.[50]

This will be exemplified in the following:

---

[47] Cp. Diehl, S. (2009), p. 150.
[48] Cp. Nitzsch, R. (2006), p. 105.
[49] Cp. Akert, R.M., Aronson, E., Wilson, T. (2008), p. 16; Beckmann, J. Heckhausen, H. (2006), p. 97; Schünemann, H. (2000), p. 29; Wendt, R. (2009), p. 80.
[50] Cp. Pepels, W. (2007), p. 92; Perloff, R.M. (2003), p. 227.

A restaurant visitor has to decide between two dishes – veal or goose. After he come to the decision to order the goose he observe a guess telling that the veal is extraordinary delicious. At this moment cognitive dissonance arise and the justification process begin in order to avoid the return of the dish. He devaluate the advantages of the veal by telling that the veal is almost looking burnt. At the same time he upgrade the disadvantages of the goose by telling that it is the best he have ever eat. Another possibility is to ignore guest's statement or to search for other guests, who are satisfied with the goose too and thus confirm his decision.[51]

This example illustrates, that humans apply to methods to reduce this emotional state, instead of confess having made a wrong decision, which in turn result into regret.

Influencing factors, which strengthen or weaken the cognitive dissonance are the grade of responsibility, involvement, commitment, importance, irreversibility and similarity of the alternatives, which is named cognitive overlap.[52]

2.2.3.2. Regret Avoidance

As already mentioned, decisions are implicated by positive and negative consequences. Positive outcomes make humans feel proud whereas bad outcomes make them feel regret and place them under pressure to justify their made decisions. This in turn increases human's cognitive dissonance. Therefore they avoid those situations respectively are regret averse.[53]

This anomaly leads to the omission bias and status quo bias. More detailed, humans tend to remain passive as consequences of actively made decisions lead to stronger regret than for similar consequences, which result from passivity. It also comes to the disposition effect, namely humans are more willing to realize gains than losses.[54]

This will be demonstrated in the following example:

An investor buys a share, which does not show any movement. Although he has been advised to sell it he remains inactive respectively hold it as he fears to fell regret about subsequent stock price increases. Additionally, upon loss realization he has to confess, that he made a wrong decision, which in turn results in an increase in cognitive disso-

---

[51] Cp. Goldberg, J., Nitzsch, R. (2004), p. 120.
[52] Cp. Berndt, R. (1996), p. 78; Conze, O. (2007), p. 31; Florissen, A. (2005), p. 173.
[53] Cp. Hadani, E.I., Holtfort, T. (2009), p. 568-574.
[54] Cp. Drabe, K., Kondert, K., Lippert, T., Neusel, T., Schirp, W. (2009), p. 104; Wunderle, S. (2006), p. 48.

nance. Contrary shares, which show a good performance will be sold too early in order to avoid the pressure to justify subsequent stock price decreases and hence the feeling of regret.[55]

This example illustrates, that humans behave risk seeking in loss situations and risk avers in gain situations.

A factor, which strengthen this irrationality is the importance and severity of decisions.[56]

2.2.3.3. Overconfidence Bias

Humans overestimate their abilities and knowledge as well as the accuracy and reliability of information. This overestimation respectively overconfidence makes humans believe, that their made decisions are correctly and reliable.[57]

This anomaly facilitates the decision making and thus is comparable to the functions, which the already mentioned heuristics fulfil. Thereby it leads to negligence in decision making, namely no further information are generated in order to check the accuracy of the made decisions. This denial happens, because humans do not challenge their own decisions as they attach them too much value and quality. Additionally, they dislike to confess loosing control due to cognitive dissonance. In contrary, they insist and adhere on their decisions and hence no amendments will be made, which results for instance to a delayed break off of a project. This in turn leads to a slowed and deformed learning process. Moreover, easy accessible as well as representative information contribute to the neglect of further information and leads to overconfidence too.[58]

A manifestation of this anomaly is the hindsight bias, which is human's overestimation of their forecasting abilities. More detailed, they regard a past event as predictable, which leads to an overestimation of their forecasting abilities. A further appearance is the self attribution bias. Several by accident arising successes confirm and strengthen humans´ made decisions. These successes will in turn be attributed to the own abilities

[55] Cp. Wunderle, S. (2006), p. 48.
[56] Cp. http://docs.google.com/viewer?a=v&q=cache:-bh337rDmJIJ:www.iew.uzh.ch/study/courses /downloads/behfin04.pdf, dated on 08.02.2011.
[57] Cp. Globocnik, D. (2011), p. 99; Langer, T. (1999), p. 13; Schmeisser, W. (2010), p. 261; Wiswede, G. (2007), p. 32.
[58] Cp. Liekweg, A. (2003), p. 279; Myers, D.G. (2008), p. 438; Weber, M. (2007), p. 38.

and knowledge whereas failings will be assigned to the fortuitousness. Thereby control illusion and decreasing risk sensitiveness arise.[59]

This will be illustrated on the following example:

The success or flop of a newly introduced product depends on the abilities and knowledge of the entrepreneur respectively its competitiveness as well as on external factors. A success will be attributed to the own capabilities and knowledge whereas a flop will be attributed to external factors. Both scenarios lead to a slowed learning process as well as to overconfidence and control illusion. Further examples are human's overestimation of their driving abilities and punctual accomplishment of a project respectively underestimation of time available.[60]

A factor, which strengthen this irrationality is the exaggerated optimism as well as the increasing severity of decisions.[61]

The behavioural anomalies mentioned in this chapter influence the development of capital markets, i.e. are explanations for the capital market anomalies respectively phenomena, which will be described in the following.

---

[59] Cp. Bergold, U., Mayer, B. (2005), 26; Bortenländer, C., Kirstein, U. (2009), p. 352; Kommer, G. (2001), p. 190; Rudolph, B. (2006), p. 152.
[60] Cp. Weber, M. (2007), p. 40-41; http://docs.google.com/viewer?a=v&q=cache:-bh337rDmJIJ: www.iew.uzh.ch/study/courses/downloads/behfin04.pdf, dated on 08.02.2011.
[61] Cp. Jörg Perrin, P. (2007), p. 46.

3. Capital Market Anomalies/Phenomena

Capital market anomalies are abnormal deviations on the capital market, which can't be sufficiently explained with the traditional capital market theory. To these phenomena belong the calendar anomalies, figure anomalies and market efficiency anomalies.[62]

3.1. Calendar Anomalies

Calendar anomalies are also known as seasonal effects. These effects induce higher yields, e.g. of shares in certain months or weekdays in comparison to other months or weekdays. Calendar anomalies contradict the random-walk hypothesis and lead to capital market inefficiencies. The most famous anomalies are the weekend effect, the January effect and the turn-of-the-month effect.[63]

3.1.1. Weekend Effect

The weekend effect is also known as the Monday effect or the day-of-the-week effect. This anomaly involves abnormal negative or low yields on Mondays than on the remaining weekdays.[64]

The rational explanation for this effect is the timing of company news releases. Companies tend to publish negative news about the development of their companies on Friday, shortly before the stock exchange market closes whereas positive information will be provided immediately. Companies assume, that market participants will forget these negative information during the weekend. However, this company strategy hasn't been proved as successfully, as most of the market participants take their decisions on weekends, which results in the sale of their shares on Monday and hence to an increase in supply. This in turn leads to a decrease of the stock prices on that day.[65]

The irrational explanation for this phenomenon is market participant's risk sensitiveness. More precisely, they dislike to expose their investments to the uncertainty of the weekend. Therefore they sell their shares on Friday, which leads to a stock price de-

---

[62] Cp. Lies, J.J. (2003), p. 180.
[63] Cp. Hauser, S.E. (2003), p. 56; Heckmann, T. (2009), p. 147; Holtfort, T. (2009), p. 50; Montassér, R.D. (2003), p. 11.
[64] Cp. Rudolph, B. (2006), p. 146.
[65] Cp. Copeland, T.E., Shastri, K., Weston, J.F. (2008), p. 504;.http://www.finanzentest.de/lexikon/1770/ Wochenendeffekt.html, dated on 08.02.2011.

crease on that day and which in turn will be reflected on the first trading day - the Monday. Another behavioural explanation is market participant's decreasing optimism. Underperformed shares as well as shares, which indicate high volatility on Friday lead to a decrease of market participant's optimism, i.e. their probability estimations concerning a stock price increase or a recovery in volatility is low. Therefore they sell their shares on Friday, which leads to a deduction of the stock prices on Monday. Mental accounting is a further human anomaly, which supply the explanation for this effect. This human anomaly states, that market participants create different mental accounts for each week. In this sense, they regard Fridays as a settlement of a mental account whereas Mondays implicate an opening of a new mental account. Another psychological reason is market participant's motivation after the weekend, which can be compared to human's motivation on its first working day. Their relaxing mood still exists on Monday, which results in low trading volumes and hence negative or low stock prices on this specific day.[66]

3.1.2. January Effect

The January effect is also known as the turn-of-the-year effect. This effect describes the phenomenon, that above-average yields will be recorded in January rather than in the remaining eleven months of the year.[67]

The outperformance in January will be explained by economical reasons like tax motives or window dressing. Easily explained, market participants sell underperformed shares at the end of the year. Hence they realize losses, which are tax deductable. These capital losses will be offset with the high yields, which will be achieved through the reinvestment in shares in January. This transaction refers also to good performed shares. In this case, market participants sell shares at the end of the year, but with the ulterior motive to save taxes. In January they reinvests their capital, which they obtained through its sale. Window dressing concerns rather institutional investors than private market participants. They sell risky shares in December in order to obtain a better looking end-of-year balance sheet. These risky shares will be purchased again in January. All scenarios lead to a stock price increase respectively high yields in January. Another

---

[66] Cp. Fields, M.J. (1931), p. 415; Shiller, R. J. (1998), p. 9; http://issuu.com/seenplatte/docs/behavioral_finance_theorie, dated on 08.02.2011; http://www.finanz-lexikon.de/wochenend-effekt_3996.html, dated on 08.02.2011.
[67] Cp. Bak, J. (2003), p. 41; Stark, G. (2005), p. 236.

explanation are bonuses and other gratifications, which market participants obtain at the end of the year and which they use for new investments in January.[68]

Aside from economical reasons, there exists a psychological reason, which explains this phenomenon too. The behavioural explanation is market participant's irrationality, named mental accounting. This human anomaly states, that market participants create different mental accounts for each year. In this sense, they regard the December as a settlement of a mental account whereas January implicates an opening of a new mental account.[69]

3.1.3. Turn-of-the-Month Effect

The turn-of-the-month effect induces high stock prices at the end of a month and at the beginning of the following month.[70]

The reason for this anomaly is market participant's solvency. More in detail, they obtain their loans and interest yields from their investments at the end of the month respectively at the beginning of the month. This leads to an increase in demand for new investments and hence to an increase in stock prices. However, in the course of the month market participant's liquidity decreases, which in turn results in the sale of their shares. This again leads to an increased supply and decreased demand on the capital market and hence to a stock price decrease in the course of the month.[71]

The behavioural explanation for this phenomenon is human's irrationality, named mental accounting. This human anomaly states, that market participants create different mental accounts for each month. In this sense, they regard the last month as a settlement of a mental account whereas the new month implicates an opening of a new mental account.[72]

Further calendar anomalies, which will be not explained in detail are the summer effect respectively the sell-in-may-and-go-away strategy, which induces high yields from October to April; the time-of-the-day effect respectively the intra-day effect, which indi-

---

[68] Cp. Parness, M. (2006), p. 188; Siegel, J.J. (2008), p. 310; http://smartinmoney.com/january_ effect.aspx, dated on 08.02.2011.

[69] Cp. Shiller, R. J. (1998), p. 9.

[70] Cp. Markellos, R.N., Mills, T.C. (2008), p. 156.

[71] Cp. Kogan, P. (2009), p. 10.

[72] Cp. Shiller, R. J. (1997), p. 9.

cates, that high yields will be achieved at the beginning and at the end of a trading day; and the holiday effect, which states, that high yields will be recorded before holidays.[73]

3.2. Figure Anomalies

Figure anomalies refer to fundamentals, i.e. induce abnormal deviations, which depend on fundamentals. To these anomalies belong the size effect, the neglected-firm effect, the book-to-market-ratio effect as well as the price-earnings-ratio effect.[74]

3.2.1. Size Effect and Neglected-Firm Effect

The size effect is also known as the small-firm effect. This anomaly leads to the fact, that companies, which indicate a low market capitalization record higher risk-adjusted yields in the long-term than those, which indicate a high market capitalization.[75]

The rational explanation for this effect is the neglected-firm effect. This effect indicates higher yields of companies, which are not observed by analysts – small caps – in comparison to those, which are focused – large caps. Its negligence results in low information transparency respectively lack of information about these companies. This leads to higher uncertainty and higher risks, which will be compensated by higher yields. Another explanation is the long-term growth potential of small sized companies in comparison to those of large sized companies. A further reason for this effect is the low dividend payment of small caps, which in turn will be invested into their growth and hence contributes to higher yields in the long-term. Additionally, small caps are more prone to financial distress especially in bear market situations, due to its high volatility and low liquidity, which will also be indemnified with higher yields. The last explanation is that small caps are more prone to mergers and acquisitions, which will be compensated with higher yields too.[76]

The psychological explanation for this effect is the anchor heuristic as well as availability heuristic. Due to limited information about small caps they revise more slowly their expectations, which leads to higher yields in the long-term. Another irrational explana-

---

[73] Cp. Duggan, M. (1999), p. 533; http://www.ad-hoc-news.de/sell-in-may-effekt--/de/Boersenlexikon/16332716, dated on 08.02.2011.
[74] Cp. Zajonz, R. (2010), p. 188.
[75] Cp. Horne, J.C., Wachowicz, J.M. (2005), p. 112; Stark, G. (2005), p. 236.
[76] Cp. Kiehling, H. (2001), p. 133; Oetken, P. (2010), p. 48-49; Pradhuman, S.D. (2000), p. 37ff, http://thismatter.com/money/investments/market-anomalies.htm, dated on 08.02.2011

tion is market participant's risk sensitiveness. More precisely, they undervalue risks of large caps in comparison to those of small caps. However, upon recognition of the reversed case, they adjust they beliefs, which leads to higher yields of small caps in the long-term.[77]

3.2.2. Book-to-Market-Ratio Effect

Another term for this effect is the value effect. The book-to-market-ratio is a financial figure, which will be used to evaluate company's market value, while comparing its market value with its book value. The book value indicates the sum of company's assets respectively its net assets, which will be derived from the balance sheet whereas the market value indicates the stock price of a company on the capital market.[78]

This effect indicates high yields of company shares, which have a high book-to-market-ratio respectively the book value is higher than the market value (value shares) in comparison to those, which indicate a low book-to-market-ratio respectively the book value is lower than the market value (growth shares). Shares, which indicate a book-to-market-ratio lower one are stated as value shares whereas those, which indicate a book-to-market-ratio above one are stated as growth shares.[79]

The rational explanation for this effect are the risks, which low book-to-market-ratio company shares involve and which will be compensated by high yields.[80]

The psychological explanation for the temporary overvaluation of growth shares and undervaluation of value shares is market participant's tendency to extrapolate good or bad performances into the future. This leads to a short-term overvaluation of good performed growth shares and an undervaluation of bad performed value shares. A further behavioural explanation is market participant's mental anchor and hence reference point. Their set reference point is the book value and thus they interpret a high book value as a growth potential. This motivate them to invest into those undervalued shares, which leads to increased stock prices and thus higher yields in the long-term. Another explanation is framing. A high book value signals future growth potential. Optimism

---

[77] Cp. Roll, R. (1981), p. 879-888; http://papers.ssrn.com/sol3/papers.cfm?abstract_id=952472, dated on 08.02.2011.
[78] Cp. North, K. (2005), p. 232.
[79] Cp. Himmelreich, A. (2006), p. 113; http://www.boersenpoint.de/blog/borsenstrategien-value-growth-strategie/, dated on 08.02.2011.
[80] Cp. Fama, E., French, K. (1993), p. 3-56.

and overconfidence arise, which leads to the purchase of value shares and thus to high yields in the long-term too.[81]

3.2.3. Price-Earnings-Ratio Effect

The price-earnings-ratio is also a financial figure, which will be used to evaluate company's market value, while comparing its market price with its expected earnings.[82]

This effect implicates, that company shares, which indicate a low price-earnings-ratio (value shares) achieve higher risk-adjusted yields in the long-term than those, which indicate a high price-earnings-ratio (growth shares). Shares, which indicate a price-earnings-ratio lower twelve are stated as value shares whereas those, which indicate a price-earnings-ratio above twenty are stated as growth shares.[83]

The rational explanation for this effect are the risks, which low price-earnings-ratio company shares involve and which will be compensated by high yields.[84]

The irrational explanation for the temporary undervaluation of low price-earnings-ratio shares is market participant's extrapolation of bad news and past negative performance, namely their mental anchor. Hence they are pessimistic about company's future earnings. Upon the announcement of new positive information they overreact, adjust their beliefs, the stock price increases and hence leads to rising yields. In contrary, market participants overvalue future returns of a company, based on good news and previously good performance. Hence they are optimistic about company's future earnings. Upon the announcement of new negative information they overreact, adjust their beliefs, the stock price falls and hence leads to decreasing yields. A further explanation for this effect is that low price-earnings-ratio shares are cheaper than high price-earnings-ratio shares, due to its undervaluation. This leads to the fact that most of the market participants purchase those low price-earnings-ratio shares, due the assumption that the ratio will revert to its trend, which leads to a stock price increase and hence to high yields in the long-term.[85]

---

[81] Cp. Hauber, R. (2002), p. 147; Pfirsching, F. (2007), p. 106; http://www.faz.net/s/Rub4B891837ECD 14082816D9E088A2D7CB4/Doc~E97563D32E2E044489D3861D3981D7D5E~ATpl~Ecommon ~Scontent.html, dated on 08.02.2011.
[82] Cp. Müller, M. (2008), p. 159.
[83] Cp. Hoose, A. (2006), p. 289; http://www.boersenpoint.de/blog/borsenstrategien-value-growth-strategie/, dated on 08.02.2011.
[84] Cp. http://thismatter.com/money/investments/market-anomalies.htm, dated on 08.02.2011.
[85] Cp. Levinson, M. (2010), p. 147; Ryland, P. (2009), p. 155.

A further figure anomaly, which will be not described in detail is the dividend-price-ratio effect, which induces high yields of shares, which indicate a high dividend yield in comparison to those, which indicate a low dividend yield.[86]

3.3. Market Efficiency Anomalies

Market efficiency anomalies are phenomena, which refute the statement, that markets are efficient. To this phenomena belong the index effect, bubbles and crashs, the home bias, the over-reaction and under-reaction, the momentum effect, the mean reversion, the announcement effect as well as the closed-end-fund puzzle.

3.3.1. Index Effect

The index effect induces abnormal market reactions respectively high share prices of financial instruments upon its index addition and low share prices upon its deletion. However, the increase or decrease in share prices does not only arise upon its index entry respectively index deletion, but shortly before, i.e. on the announcement day.[87]

The explanation for this effect is market participant's short-term portfolio adjustment. Easily explained, upon the announcement of an index addition respectively deletion they purchase these shares, which will be added to the index and sell those, which are intended to be deleted. This leads to a short-term surplus demand of those shares, which will be added to the index and to a short-term surplus supply of those, which will be deleted. This in turn results in positive or high respectively negative or low stock prices. This shifting implicates a temporary index effect.[88]

Aside from a temporary index effect it exists a permanent index effect too. The explanation for a positive permanent index effect is the increase on information available, which arises due to an index entry. This results in lower risk premiums, which in turn leads to an increase of share prices and hence a positive permanent index effect. Contrary, a permanent negative index effect arises, due to an index deletion. The quantity of information available decreases and hence market participants request higher risk premiums. This leads to a decrease of share prices and hence a negative permanent index

---

[86] Cp. http://docs.google.com/viewer?a=v&q=cache:nveOPEhDWe4J:www.isb.uzh.ch/publikationen /pdf/publ_2005.pdf, dated on 08.02.2011.
[87] Cp. Friebel, M. (2010), p. 33.
[88] Cp. Schmidt-Tank, S. (2005), p. 64.

effect. Another explanation for a permanent positive or negative index effect is that shares, which entered or left the index are not available respectively available on the market in the long-term. This leads to a decrease respectively increase in supply and hence increase respectively decrease of stock prices.[89]

The index effect will be explained by market participant's irrationality too. The behavioural anomaly, named mental accounting leads to a different evaluation of the indexes. In other words, if a share enters an index market participants allocate it to another mental account, which they created for shares, which belong to this index. This account will be newly evaluated, which deviates from the evaluation of the other accounts. This in turn leads to a wrong evaluation of the values of the indexes and hence an index effect. Another explanation is market participant's risk sensitiveness and framing, namely an index entry signals stability and high returns based on which risk sensitiveness decreases whereas an index deletion signal instability and low returns based on which risk sensitiveness increases. Final explanation is the availability heuristic, which will be applied to due lack of information of companies, which left an index and increase of information of companies, which entered the index.[90]

3.3.2. Bubbles and Crashs

Bubbles and crashs will be expressed by excessively price increases respectively price decreases for instance of raw materials, shares or real estates, which extremely deviate from its real fundamental value.[91]

The formation and collapse of a bubble consists of five steps and will be explained by market participant's irrationality. The bubble begins with a positive external shock, which leads to an initial increase in stock prices and yields. This trend reversal will be recognized by some market participants and hence motivate them to start an investment. Further arising stock price increases, which meet and confirm market participant's expectations lead to further stock price increases as well as high returns and yield achievements. This in turn invite further market participants to enter the market in order to participate on further rising stock prices. Meanwhile market participants assume this development as representative and extrapolate this performance into the future. Accom-

---

[89] Cp. http://docs.google.com/viewer?a=v&q=cache:FuTxj2GJcGwJ:joergfleischer.com/Publikationen/ Indexeffekt.PDF, dated on 08.02.2011.
[90] Cp. Shiller, R. J. (1997), p. 9.
[91] Cp. http://www.zzzzz.de/lexikon/s/sp/spekulationsblase.html, dated on 08.02.2011.

panied by market participant's herding behaviour a trend arises, which boost the stock prices too. Additionally, published positive expert opinions strengthen their behaviour. They become overly optimistic and euphoric. Driven by gear, wishful thinking, control illusion and overconfidence to obtain short-term high returns and yields they ignore warning signals respectively the risk sensitiveness decreases. In this stage they are ready to pay a higher price, which deviates from its real value. This behaviour is called the winner's curse, which can be compared to an auction, where participants bet with higher prices in order to obtain the good. In the meantime the stock price has been deviated far apart from its fundamental value, i.e. the raw material, share or real estate has been overvalued, which leads to a bubble on the capital market.[92]

The crash begins due to a negative external shock, which leads to an initial reverse or stagnation in stock prices and yields. Due to market participant's loss aversion they do not react immediately. However, further stock price declines motivate them to short-sell their investments, as the risks overvalue the yields. Meanwhile they begin to recognize the overvaluation of the raw material, share or real estate and hence fear further losses, which lead to a mass short-sell respectively panic. This in turn results in an excessively stock price decrease below its fundamental value, i.e. to a crash on the capital market.[93]

3.3.3. Home Bias

Home bias is a capital market anomaly, which arises due to home market's overvaluation caused by market participant's preference to invest in home markets rather than in foreign markets.[94]

Economical reasons, which explain this phenomenon are transaction costs, exchange rate risks, political risks, market access restrictions as well as taxation.[95]

Behavioural explanations for this anomaly are framing, risk sensitiveness, overconfidence, ambiguity aversion as well as the availability heuristic. Explained in detail, domestic market participants have a better access to home market-based information rather than to foreign market-based information. Additionally, domestic information are perspicuously understandable, as they will be provided in domestic language. Domestic

---

[92] Cp. Vogt, G. (2009), p. 363-365.
[93] Cp. http://docs.google.com/viewer?a=v&q=cache:qIzmbSiI-s4J:www.oliverfaulhaber.de/talks/ Seminar_2008_FSS.pdf, dated on 08.02.2011.
[94] Cp. Raab, G. (2006), p. 113.
[95] Cp. Bouchet, M.H., Clark, E., Groslambert, B. (2003), p. 157.

newspapers as well as media increase the information flow and hence contribute to an easier mental information retrieval. This results in a stronger perception of information with a high subjective ratio, irrespectively, if they are more important than other information. This in turn will additionally be strengthen by the way how those information will be demonstrated, i.e. framed. The more information are available the more overconfidence they get and hence results in a decreased risk sensitiveness. This will additionally be strengthen, if market participants or somebody in their environments are engaged for this domestic company or living next to it. All these factors lead to familiarity and to the belief of the ability to control the domestic market. Overconfidence and control illusion result in turn to an underestimation of risks involved and overestimation of expected gains of the home market. Moreover, lack of foreign market-based information contributes to market participant's ambiguity aversion. An investment in foreign markets leads to an increase in uncertainty, which in turn results in loss of control and hence to an increased risk sensitiveness. Therefore they have the tendency to invest in markets, which risk factors are known and assessable – domestic market - instead in markets, which risk factors are uncertain and unratable – foreign market.[96]

All those factors lead to the home bias, which in turn results in the neglect of less familiar, but markets with good prospects.

3.3.4. Over-reaction and Under-reaction

An over-reaction and under-reaction on capital markets reflects market participant's response to information. An over-reaction denotes too high or too low stock prices caused by too strong reactions on either positive or negative information. An under-reaction denotes delayed stock price movements caused by delayed reactions on either positive or negative information.[97]

Market participant's response to information will be explained by anomalies in their information perception and information processing process. An over-reaction will be caused by framing, overconfidence, the availability heuristic and representative heuristic. Vividly and sudden published information are more available and easier assessable in market participant's minds. These recently positive or negative information will be assumed as more probable and representative. Hence market participants rely on recent

---

[96] Cp. Jörg Perrin, P. (2007), p. 90; Kottke, N. (2005), p. 201; Rudolph, B. (2006), p. 151.
[97] Cp. Burghardt, R., Werner, T. (2006), p. 34.

information and overconfidently extrapolate them into the future. They think to recognize a trend, which they follow. This trend will in turn be strengthen by herding. All these anomalies lead to an immediate information processing, which results in an over-reaction on the capital market. This over-reaction results in a short-term till middle-term momentum effect and a subsequent long-term mean reversion effect, which will be explained in 3.3.5. and 3.3.6.[98]

An under-reaction will be induced by anchoring, selective perception, overconfidence, confirmation bias, regret and loss aversion as well as gambler's fallacy. Market participants orientate and adhere to their private information even though they are contrary. Consequently, public information will be under-valued and neglected, as they contradict their conceptions. This results in an incomplete adjustment of their mental anchor. Additionally, previous investment successes lead to overconfidence and result in the neglect of contrary information too. On the other hand, previous investment failings lead to regret and loss avoidance. Market participants fear to feel regret about decisions, which will subsequently been proved as faulty or losses. A further irrationality is market participant's belief, that current deviations will be evened out by opposite deviations in the future. All these anomalies lead to a temporary status quo and hence to a delayed information processing, which results in an under-reaction on the capital market. Also the under-reaction leads to a short-term till middle-term momentum effect and a subsequent long-term mean reversion effect, which will be described in the following.[99]

3.3.5. Momentum Effect

The momentum effect involves a short-term till middle-term positive or negative yield continuation. More detailed, e.g. shares, which achieved high or low yields in the last 3 to 12 months will record the same good or bad performance in the future, i.e. next 6 to 12 months. This effect is also known as pro-cyclical trend, namely market participants purchase for instance shares, which indicate an increasing stock price and short-sell

---

[98] Cp. Kowalewski, J. (2008), p. 107; Külpmann, M. (2004), p. 121; Wärneryd, K.E. (2001), p. 158; http://docs.google.com/viewer?a=v&q=cache:2svPfNsVNcgJ:www.commendo.de/rw_e7v/commendo2/usr_documents/Nitzsch_Aufsatz_Behavioral-Finance.pdf, dated on 08.02.2011; http://docs.google.com/viewer?a=v&q=cache:j8GLqOv_WuUJ:www.efi.rwth-aachen.de/downloads/Forschung/WorkingPaper/workingpaper2009-01.pdf, dated on 08.02.2011.

[99] Cp. Atrill, P. (2009), p. 276; Baker, H.K., Nofsinger, J.R. (2010), p. 704; Jones, R.C. (1998), p. 76; Redhead, K. (2008), p. 499; Sewell, M. (2011), p. 211; http://docs.google.com/viewer?a=v&q=cache:3HiLHtToOEwJ:finanzportal.wiwi.uni-saarland.de/behav/boom_bust.PDF, dated on 08.02.2011.

those, which indicate a decreasing stock price. This behaviour contributes that winners remain winners and losers remain losers.[100]

As already mentioned, this effect arises, due to an over-reaction as well as a an under-reaction on the capital market induced by market participant's response to new public information.[101]

A momentum effect caused by an under-reaction to new information arises due to market participant's mental anchor and selective perception. More detailed, they refer to past events such like prior high or low company returns. This good or bad company performance will be extrapolated into the future. This leads to the neglect of new public contrary information, adherence of old information and hence missing adjustment, i.e. update of their mental anchor. Based on their non updated mental anchor they anticipate the same good or bad development in the future and thus purchase good performed shares and short-sell bad performed shares. This will be strengthen by overconfidence and self-attribution bias. As market participants are certain on their own knowledge and analytical abilities they neglect new public contrary information. Also in this case they anticipate the same good or bad development in the future and thus they purchase good performed shares and short-sell bad performed shares. This in turn will additionally be strengthen by herding. These anomalies implicate a delayed information processing, which in turn leads to a trend prolongation respectively momentum, i.e. winners remain winners and losers remain losers.[102]

A momentum effect due to an over-reaction to new information is caused by the representative heuristic and availability bias. Conversely to the under-reaction where market participants overvalue previous private information and undervalue new public information in this case market participants overvalue new public information and undervalue past private information. They belief to notice a trend, which they follow and extrapolate this new information into the future – close to the motto a trend is your friend. Market participants become optimistic about recent winners and pessimistic about recent losers and hence they purchase good performed shares and short-sell bad performed shares. This will be strengthen by overconfidence and self-attribution bias, which arise,

---

[100] Cp. Geier, C. (2009), p. 14; Holtfort, T., Nelles, M., Uzik, M. (2007), p. 444; Kontrec-Goedecke, M. (2010), p. 55; Spremann, K. (2006), p. 42.

[101] Cp. Becker, A. (2009), p. 447.

[102] Cp. Arnold, G. (2008), p. 576; Daniel, K., Hirshleifer, D., Subrahmanyam, A. (1998), p. 1842 ff; Weber, M. (2007), p. 83; http://docs.google.com/viewer?a=v&q=cache:W5eUVZua5toJ:badger.som.yale.edu/faculty/ncb25/bsv_nonac.pdf, dated on 08.02.2011.

if new public information are in context with their private information. Also these anomalies implicate a delayed information processing, which in turn leads to a trend prolongation respectively momentum, i.e. winners remain winners and losers remain losers.[103]

The momentum effect results in the mean reversion effect, which will be described in the following.

3.3.6. Mean Reversion Effect

The mean reversion effect or winner-loser effect is the tendency for instance of stock prices to return in the long-term to its average respectively mean after a short-term till middle-term phase of overstatement or understatement. More detailed, good performed shares will achieve lower yields and bad performed shares will achieve higher yields in the future. This effect is also known as anti-cyclical trend, namely market participants purchase for instance shares, which indicate a decreasing stock price and short-sell those, which indicate an increasing stock price.[104]

The explanation for this effect is market participant's risk sensitiveness. Easily explained, the indeed development does not correspond to market participant's investment behaviour. Due to contrary or lack of confirming information they recognize that winners are not winners and that losers are not losers. Hence, they revise their investment behaviour, which results in a long-term mean reversion respectively stock price correction. Another explanation is gambler's fallacy. Market participants anticipate that stock price increases are followed by stock price decreases and in reverse - close to the motto what goes up comes down. Therefore they tend to sell long-term increasing shares and to purchase long-term decreasing shares. This effect will be strengthen by herding behaviour. More detailed, market participants follow other market participants, i.e. if they purchase or sell a share they purchase or sell a share too. These anomalies results in a

---

[103] Cp. De Bondt, W.F.M., Thaler, R. H. (1984), p. 793-805; Haas, A., Scheufele, B. (2008), p. 64; http://docs.google.com/viewer?a=v&q=cache:52eIIfa7NHoJ:www.belkcollege.uncc.edu/dashapir/ SeminarPhDClass8.pdf, dated on 08.02.2011; http://www.duke.edu/~gwc/Behavioral%20 explanations%20for%20short.htm, dated on 08.02.2011; http://webcache.googleusercontent.com /search?q=cache:XhTsyDzLlTkJ:www.isb.uzh.ch/publikationen/pdf/2747.pdf, dated on 08.02.2011; http://docs.google.com/viewer?a=v&q=cache:K34308SjPb0J:www.behavioral finance.ch/domains/behavioralfinance_ch/data/Catalog/101008/ZuerichFinNeu.pdf, dated on 08.02.2011.

[104] Cp. Aschoff, H. (2006), p.30; Kiell, G., Moerschen, T. (2003), p. 87; Kogan, P. (2009), p. 18.

long-term mean reversion, i.e. previous winners achieve lower yields and become losers whereas previous losers achieve higher yields and become winners.[105]

3.3.7. Announcement Effect

The announcement of an event such like an increase in capital leads to abnormal reactions on the capital market respectively arising price deviations, which have been caused by an announcement. These deviations occur with time delay respectively still exist after the announcement day.[106]

Stock price deviations reflect the information value. Thus an announcement is a signal – either in a positive or negative way – and influences market participant's decisions, either to invest or to disinvest for instance in shares. This in turn leads to stock price movements, either in a negative or in a positive way.[107]

The explanation for the announcement effect is market participant's information processing process. Upon the announcement, they process new information respectively they adjust their prior anchor, which leads to a delayed information processing. This in turn depends on market participant's expectations, which influence the strength of this effect. In other words, the strength of the announcement effect depends on market participant's probability estimations. The more probable they anticipated the occurrence of this event and hence its announcement the lower the announcement effect will arise. In contrast, the more surprised they have been by the event occurrence and hence its announcement the stronger it will arises. Another irrationality is mental accounting. In other words, upon the announcement of a capital increase they allocate it to another mental account, which they created for capital increases only. This account will be newly evaluated, which deviates from the evaluation of the other accounts. This leads to a wrong evaluation and hence to the announcement effect. These anomalies result in a drag on of price deviations caused by the announcement and hence to the announcement effect.[108]

---

[105] Cp. De Bondt, W.F.M., Thaler, R. H. (1989), p. 189-202; Kiehling, H. (2001), p. 130 ff; Kiell, G., Moerschen, T. (2003), p. 90; http://issuu.com/seenplatte/docs/behavioral_finance_theorie, dated on 08.02.2011.
[106] Cp. http://docs.google.com/viewer?a=v&q=cache:p5ZyTMkbqp8J:www1.uni-hamburg.de/Kapitalmaerkte/download/SeminarWiSe200304Folien7.pdf, dated on 08.02.2011.
[107] Cp. Bitz, M., Stark, G. (2008), p. 233.
[108] Cp. Bott, C. (2002), p. 306, 361.

3.3.9. Closed-End Fund Puzzle

The closed-end fund puzzle is also known as the discount paradox. This anomaly leads to the effect, that the market price of a closed-end fund does not reflect its real value respectively its net asset value. More precisely, closed-end fund shares are sell at prices, which are not equal to their net asset value.[109]

This phenomenon will be explained by the supply and demand on the capital market, which determine the market price as well as by the discount, which arises during its duration. The anomaly consists of four puzzles. At the outset it will be traded at a premium to its net asset value, which arises, due to high demand and which leads to an increase in its market price and a decrease in its net asset value. Thereafter it will be traded at a discount to its net asset value, due to low demand and which leads to a decrease in its market price and an increase in its net asset value. Afterwards discount volatilities arise. In the last step of the puzzle the closed-end-fund will be liquidated or converted into an open-end-fund, which leads to a market price decrease and to a shrinking discount, but which not fully disappears. Hence a premium arises, if the market price is above the net asset value whereas a discount arises, if the market price is below the net asset value.[110]

The economical explanation for the existence of the discount are transaction costs, administration costs, agency costs as well as tax reasons. Further explanations are risks, which a closed-end fund implicates, due to its illiquidity and low fungibility.[111]

Besides of rational explanations there exist also behavioural explanations for its existence. One irrational reason is market participant's selective perception and mental anchor. Expressed in other words, they neglect the net asset value and observe or orient only on the market price. This leads to discount volatilities and hence deviations between the market price and the net asset value. Another psychological reason is market participant's sentiment respectively their expectations about future returns, which have an impact on the demand and the volatility of the discounts and hence results in deviations between the market price and the net asset value. A pessimistic attitude towards future developments leads to high discounts whereas an optimistic attitude results in

---

[109] Cp. Lee, C.M.C., Shleifer, A., Thaler, R.H. (1991), 75-109.
[110] Cp. Götte, R. (2001), p. 57; Lüscher-Marty, M. (2008), p. 2.28; http://docs.google.com/viewer?a= v&q=cache:b_kNxI969YcJ:www.isb.uzh.ch/publikationen/pdf/publ_1355.pdf, dated on 08.02.2011.
[111] Cp. http://docs.google.com/viewer?a=v&q=cache:cDH8B5SHdv8J:www.mtholyoke.edu/acad/ econ/muturi.ppt, dated on 08.02.2011

low discounts. These anomalies lead to discount volatilities and hence to deviations between the market price and net asset value.[112]

Other market efficiency anomalies, which will be not explained in detail are the equity premium puzzle, which induces high yields of shares, which involve high volatilities and hence risks; and the excess volatility, which implicates too big changes respectively too high volatilities in stock prices compared to the changes of their fundamentals.[113]

---

[112] Cp. Lee, C.M.C., Shleifer, A., Thaler, R.H. (1991), 75-109; Raab, G. (2006), p. 113.
[113] Cp. http://docs.google.com/viewer?a=v&q=cache:1WfbFcdiEs0J:www.gp.tu-berlin.de/ Users/j/jungermann/Publications/WISU27.Equity_Premium.pdf, dated on 08.02.2011; http://docs.google.com/viewer?a=v&q=cache:rcT5jfR-k4J:www.suche.stiftungen.org/files/original /galerie_vom_12.02.2007_14.45.46/AssetManagement_Lunchmeeting_HSH_Nordbank_Prof._Dr. _Ruediger_von_Nitzsch.pdf, dated on 08.02.2011.

4. Empirical Evidence to the Capital Market Anomalies/Phenomena

The capital market anomalies described in chapter three were subjected to several studies, which provided the evidence for its existence as well as confirmed the insufficient explanatory power of the classical capital market theory. These studies will be presented in the following.

4.1. Empirical Evidence to the Calendar Anomalies

This part of the thesis will evidence the weekend effect on international markets followed by general empirical studies, which cover the evidence of the remaining calendar anomalies too.

4.1.1. Weekend Effect evidenced on International Markets

The first economist, who detected this seasonal pattern was French, who researched the American stock market on the basis of the S&P 500 from 1953 to 1977. He recorded a negative average yield of minus 0.1681 percent on Mondays whereas the remaining weekdays recorded positive yields. His results have been confirmed by further economists, who examined the same index. One of those was Cross. He observed a daily negative average yield of minus 0.18 percent on Mondays from 1953 to 1970. Further economists were Gibbons and Hess, who spot a daily negative average yield of minus 0.134 percent on Mondays between 1962 and 1978. Similar results have been reported by Rogalski, who investigated this effect from 1979 to 1984. He discovered a daily negative average yield of minus 0.1315 percent on Mondays. Further studies of Keim and Stambough between 1928 and 1982 detected a daily negative average yield of minus 0.186 percent. Jaffe and Westerfield supported these findings. They discovered a daily negative average yield of minus 0.13 percent from 1928 to 1983. Kamara investigated the market from 1961 to 1993. Within three sub-periods he spot a daily negative average yield of minus 0.156 percent, minus 0.043 and minus 0.033 percent. Berument and Kiymaz recorded a daily negative average yield of minus 0.0028 percent between 1973 and 1997. The last economist, named Schwert analyzed the market between 1928 and

2002. Within three sub-periods he discovered a daily negative average yield of minus 0.30 percent, minus 0.23 and minus 0.05 percent.[114]

This effect has also been examined on the British stock market by the economist Steeley from 1991 to 1998. Contrary to the studies referring the American stock market, he spot a daily positive average yield of 0.0044 percent on Mondays, which has almost been identical to the positive yields of the remaining weekdays. He stated, that this effect depends on the market situation. More in detail, a positive market situation induces positive yields on Mondays and thus no weekend effect exists whereas a negative market situation leads to negative yields on Mondays and hence to a weekend effect.[115]

Krämer and Runde investigated the German stock market between 1960 and 1989. Within this observation period their results corresponded to the results of the American studies. However, since 1990 a weak or even no weekend effect has been recorded.[116]

Theurillat researched this effect on the Swiss stock market from 1974 to 1991. He identified a daily negative yield on Mondays as well as on Tuesdays.[117]

This has also been recorded on the Italian stock market by Barone between 1975 and 1989. The yields on Tuesdays recorded a negative performance of minus 0.1874 percent whereas Mondays amounted to minus 0.1069 percent.[118]

Balaban investigated the Turkish stock market between 1988 and 1994. He spot a daily negative average yield of minus 0.030 percent on Tuesdays. Contrary, Mondays recorded a daily positive average yield of 0.086 percent.[119]

A negative yield on Tuesdays has been demonstrated by Solnik and Bousquet too, who examined the French stock market from 1978 till 1987.[120]

Jaffe and Westerfield extended their scientific researches and investigated the Japanese, Canadian, Australian and British stock market. Referring the Japanese stock market they used the Nikkei for their investigations and detected a daily negative average yield

---

[114] Cp. Berument, H., Kiymaz, H. (2001), p. 181-193; French K.R. (1980), p. 55-69; Cross, F. (1973), p. 67-69; Gibbons, M.R., Hess, P. (1981), p. 579-596; Jaffe, J.F., Westerfield, R. (1985), p. 433-454; Kamara, A. (1997), p. 63-84, sub-periods: 1962-1975, 1975-1982, 1982-1993; Keim, D.B., Stambaugh, R.F. (1984), p. 819-835; Rogalski, R.J. (1984), p. 1603-1614; Schwert, G.W. (2003), p. 939-974, sub-periods: 1928-1952, 1953-1977, 1978-2002.
[115] Cp. Steeley, J.M. (2001), p. 1941-1956.
[116] Cp. Krämer, W., Runde, R. (1997), p. 637-641; http://docs.google.com/viewer?a=v&q=cache: xmOQ4NOQr_EJ:www.wiwi.uni-muenster.de/me/downloads/Veroeffentlichungen/ SalmSiemkes.pdf, dated on 08.02.2011.
[117] Cp. Theurillat, M.J. (1996), p. 124 f.
[118] Cp. Barone, E. (1990), p. 483-510.
[119] Cp. Balaban, E. (1995), p. 139-143.
[120] Cp. Bousquet, L., Solnik, B. (1990), p. 461-468.

of minus 0.02 percent between 1970 and 1983. The Toronto stock exchange recorded a daily negative average yield of minus 0.14 percent between the sample period of 1976 and 1983. Concerning their examinations on the Australian stock market they referred to the Statex Actuaries Index and noted a daily negative average yield of minus 0.05 percent between 1973 and 1982. Regarding the British stock market they used the Financial Times Ordinary Share and examined a daily negative average yield of minus 0.14 percent from 1950 to 1983. However, more significant daily negative yields of minus 0.133 have been identified on Tuesdays in Australia and minus 0.090 percent in Japan.[121]

Another economist, who investigated this effect on emerging market was Choudhry. He examined seven Asian countries from 1990 to 1995 and discovered that five of the observed seven countries achieved negative yields on Mondays. However, some other economists, who investigated these Asian countries from 2000 to 2010 did not confirmed the results of Choudhry. Likewise Jaffe and Westerfield they recorded negative yields on Tuesdays for China, India, Indonesia, Singapore, Hong Kong, Malaysia, Philippines, Thailand and Korea.[122]

The studies concerning the weekend effect on international markets demonstrate, that this effect exists, but also that it do not arises permanently respectively depends on the market situation, shifts to other weekdays, weakens or even vanishes. An explanation for the disappearance respectively its shifting to a Tuesday effect is the American stock market, which has an impact on these markets. Easily explained, the developments on the American stock market will be reflected on these markets only on Tuesdays, due to time zone differences. A further explanation is the utilization of this strategy by market participants, which are well informed about this phenomenon, due to its publication and hence contribute to the shifting or disappearance of this effect. However, the company new releases argument do partly serves as explanation for the existence of this seasonal pattern. [123]

---

[121] Cp. Jaffe, J.F., Westerfield, R. (1985), p. 433-454.
[122] Cp. Choudhry, T. (2000), p. 235-242; Fan, X.M., Groenewold, N., Tank, S.H.K., Wu, Y. (2004), p. 55; Koh, S.-K., Wong, K.A. (2000), p. 445; Ma, S. (2004), p. 58; Siegel, J.J. (2008), p. 312.
[123] Cp. Chang, E.C., Pinegar, J.M., Ravichamdram, R. (1993), p. 497-513; Kamara, A. (1997), p. 66f; Mitchell, J.D., Ong, L.L. (2006), p. 8; http://www.faz.net/-00n82w, dated on 08.02.2011.

4.1.2. Other Studies to the remaining Calendar Anomalies

The January effect has firstly been observed by the economist Wachtel. He investigated this phenomenon in the Dow Jones Industrial Average from 1927 to 1942. Further economists, named Lakonishok and Smidt discovered the same index between 1897 and 1986 and did not confirmed the studies of Wachtel, namely they found no abnormal high yields in January, but in December. On the other hand, Schwert recognized this effect only in small sized companies from 1802 to 1987. Also Lindley et al. confirmed no permanent January effect from 1962 to 2000 and even negative yields in January. Latest studies of Moosa reconfirmed these observations, namely he detected this effect from 1970 to 1989, but not between 1990 and 2005.[124]

Rozeff and Kinney examined the New York Stock Exchange from 1904 to 1974. They observed an average yield of 3.5 percent in January whereas the remaining months recorded an average yield of only 0.5 percent. Their examinations have been confirmed by many subsequent surveys, which comprised the period from 1802 to 2005. Just like Schwert there were other economists, who detected this effect to be more significant in small sized companies rather than in large sized companies and hence supplied the explanation for the irregular observation of the January effect in the Dow Jones Industrial Average.[125]

The January effect is just like the weekend effect also an international anomaly. This has been examined by Gultekin and Gultekin from 1959 to 1979. Their reports showed, that Belgium, Denmark, Germany, Austria, France, Italy, Norway, Spain, Sweden and the Netherlands recorded above average yields in January than in the remaining months of the year. Brown et al. examined international markets, where the fiscal year does not end in December. One of those countries was Australia, where the fiscal year ends in June. From 1958 to 1981 they discovered both, a January effect and high yields in July. Further studies confirmed the same effect in countries in which the fiscal year ends in March, like England. Kato and Schallheim researched the Japanese stock market. They detected a January effect, although no capital gains have been taxable. Berges et al. dis-

---

[124] Cp. Lakonishok, J., Smidt, S. (1988), p. 403-425; Liano, K., Lindley, J., Slater, S. (2004), n/a.; Moosa, I.A. (2007), p. 92-103; Schwert, G.W. (1983), p. 3-12; Wachtel, S.B. (1942), p. 184-193.

[125] Cp. Bentzen, E., Hansson, B. (2005), p. 1-24, 1966-2002; Haug, M., Hirschey, M. (2006), p. 78-88; Haugen, R., Lakonishok, J.(1987), p. 197-212, sample period: 1927-1987; Keim, D.B. (1983), p. 13-32, sample period: 1963-1979; Reinganum, M.R. (1983), p. 89-104, sample period: 1962-1979; Rendon, J., Ziemba, W.T. (2007), p. 381-396, sample period: 1998-2005; Ritter, J.R. (1988), p. 701-717, sample period: 1970-1985; Rozeff, M.S., Kinney, W.R. (1976), p. 379-402; Schwert, G.W. (1990), p. 3-12.

covered the Canadian stock market from 1950 to 1980. They spot this effect from 1951 to 1972, although the capital gains have been taxable since 1973.[126]

The empirical results concerning the January effect show, that this effect exists and that it is much more pronounced in small sized companies. Additionally, it cannot be fully explained by tax motives and window dressing, because it occurs in countries, in which the fiscal year ends in December, but also in countries in which the fiscal year ends in other months and capital gains are not taxable. Likewise the weekend effect also this effect weakens, due to its utilization by most of the market participants caused by its publication, which in turn results in a disappearance of this effect, i.e. its shifting to other months.[127]

Another seasonal pattern is the turn-of-the-month effect, which has firstly been identified by Ariel. He investigated the American stock market based on data of the Center for Research in Security Prices between 1963 and 1981. He detected high yields on the last trading day of a month and on the first nine trading days of the subsequent month. His studies have been confirmed by Lakonishok and Smidt, who observed the Dow Jones Industrial Average from 1897 to 1987. Contrary to Ariel, they discovered this effect on the last trading day of a month and on the first three trading days of the subsequent month. The effect has been confirmed by Compton and Kunkel, who analyzed the Dow Jones Industrial Average as well as the S&P 500 from 1988 to 1997. However, their turn-of-the-month period definition included the last two trading days of a month and the first four trading days of the subsequent month. Latest surveys of McConnell and Xu reconfirmed this effect from 1987 to 2005. However, they used the same turn-of-the-month period as Lakonishok and Smidt did. Recent academic examinations, who covered the observation period from 1963 to 2008 provided its existence too and defined the same turn-of-the-month period like Lakonishok and Smidt as well as McConnell and Xu.[128]

---

[126] Cp. Berges, A., McConnell, J.J. Schlarbaum; G.G. (1984), p. 185-192; Brown, P., Kleidon, A.W., Marsh, T.A. (1983), p. 33-56; Gultekin, M.N., Gultekin, N.B. (1983), p. 469-481; Guo, Z. (2002), p. 14; Kato, K. , Schallheim, J.S. (1985), p. 243-260.
[127] Cp. Siegel, J.J. (2008), p. 310-311.
[128] Cp. Ariel, R.A. (1987), p. 161-174; Compton, W.S. Kunkel, R.A., (1998), p. 11-23; Lakonishok, J., Smidt, S. (1988), p. 403-425; McConnell, J.J., Xu, W. (2008), p. 49-64; http://docs.google.com/viewer?a=v&q=cache:Kd5KpTxHmAUJ:ir.lib.sfu.ca/dspace/bitstream/ 1892/10976/1/GAWM%25202008,%2520Ramsundhar,%2520S..pdf, dated on 08.02.2011.

The turn-of-the-month effect has been detected also on international markets. Cadsby and Ratner provided evidences for its existence in Canada, Great Britain, Australia, Switzerland and Germany from 1975 to 1989. Martikainen et al. researched this phenomenon from 1988 to 1990 and confirmed this pattern in Belgium, Germany, Canada, France, South Africa and Switzerland. However, their turn-of-the-month period has been defined as the last trading day of a month and the first four trading days of the subsequent month. Additionally, they detected high yields at the beginning of the month, but not on the last trading day of the previous month in Germany. This has been refuted by the studies of Röder, who discovered the German market between 1960 and 1992. He noticed high yields on the first three trading days, but also on the last trading day of the former month. Recent scientific studies of Beyer et al, who identified this effect in 15 of 19 countries from 1988 to 2000 supported those findings as well the turn-of-the-month period stated by Röder, Lakonishok and Smidt as well as by McConnell and Xu. Latest academic studies, which covered the observation period from 2001 to 2005 reconfirmed its existence as well as the latest definitions of the turn-of-the-month period.[129]

The surveys relating to the turn-of-the-month effect provide the evidence, that this effect exists. In spite of different turn-of-the month period definitions, latest studies prove, that high yields will be recorded on the last trading day of the month as well on the first three trading days of the subsequent month. However, studies of McConnell and Xu cannot fully confirm market participant's solvency as explanation for its existence.[130]

4.2. Empirical Evidence to the Figure Anomalies

This part of the thesis will evidence the size effect and neglected-firm effect on the SDAX and DAX followed by general empirical studies, which cover the evidence of the remaining figure anomalies too.

---

[129] Cp. Beyer, S., Compton, W.S., Kunkel, R.A. (2003), p. 207-221; Cadsby, C.B., Ratner, M. (1992), p. 497-509; Jaffe, J.F., Westerfield, R. (1989), p. 237-244; Martikainen, T., Perttunen, J., Ziemba, W.T. (1994), p. 41-49; Röder, K. (1994), p. 535-545; Ziemba, W.T. (1991), p. 119-146; http://ir.lib.sfu.ca/handle/1892/3412, dated on 08.02.2011.
[130] Cp. Ogden, J.P. (1990), p. 1259-1272; McConnell, J.J., Xu, W. (2008), p. 49-64.

4.2.1. Size Effect and Neglected-Firm Effect evidenced on the SDAX and DAX

This phenomenon has firstly been discovered by Banz. He investigated the American stock market between 1936 and 1975 and discovered, that small sized companies outperformed large sized companies, so called blue chips. More in detail, he compared 50 small sized caps with 50 blue chips and came to the result, that small sized companies achieved a higher yearly risk-adjusted yield of 12 percent in comparison to large sized companies. His studies have been confirmed by further economists, who researched the same market from 1926 to 1990. Studies of the Franklin Templeton Institutional confirmed the results of the economists. From 1927 to 2001 they spot an outperformance of small caps. More detailed, small caps recorded an average performance of 20 percent in comparison to large caps, which gained only 12 percent. They also noted a reversed size effect from 1990 to 1999. Within this period large caps outperformed small caps. Latest surveys of Ibbotson Associates proved this effect too. Small caps achieved a yearly risk-adjusted yield of 12.6 percent in comparison to large caps, which recorded only 10.4 percent between 1925 and 2005.[131]

Some economists noted a link between the size effect and the neglected-firm effect. Two of those were Arbel and Strebel, who analyzed the American stock market on basis of the S&P 500 from 1972 to 1976. They monitored a yearly average yield of 17.7 percent of small caps, which have been neglected by analysts. Contrary large caps, which have been focused by analysts recorded an average yield of only 6.6 percent. Carvell and Strebel analyzed the same market using the data of the Center for Research in Security Prices between 1976 and 1981. They recognized a monthly average yield of 2.4 percent of disregarded small caps whereas focused large caps, achieved an average yield of only 1.1 percent a month. This has been reconfirmed by Beard and Sias, who analyzed this effect on the American Stock Exchange from 1982 to 1995. Neglected small caps recorded a yearly average yield of 31.51 percent in comparison to blue chips, which have been focused by analysts. These caps achieved an average yield of only

---

[131] Cp. Banz, R.W. (1981), p. 3-18; Fama, E.F., French, K.R. (1992), p. 427-465, sub-period: 1963-1990; Reinganum, M.R. (1981), p. 19-46, sub-period: 1926-1981; Roll, R. (1981), p. 879-888, sub-period: 1962-1977; http://www.manager-magazin.de/finanzen/artikel/0,2828,711496-2,00.html, dated on 08.02.2011; http://docs.google.com/viewer?a=v&q=cache:w7xFfEWjjcEJ:www.ftinstitutional.ca/ca/inst/en/pdf/commentary/whitepapers/white_paper_small_caps_081804.pdf, dated on 08.02.2011.

16.59 percent a year. Also the studies of the Franklin Templeton Institutional and latest surveys of Damodaran demonstrated this link.[132]

The size effect in Germany has been researched by several economists too. One of those was Stehle, who discovered the size effect between 1954 and 1990. His results were similar to those, who examined the American stock market. More in detail, the yearly yields of small caps were 2 percent higher than those of large caps. A further economist, named Domke investigated the same market between 1971 and 1980 and confirmed this effect as well. He compared the development of the stock prices of 30 small caps with the development of the stock index of the Federal Statistical Office. The monthly average yield of small caps amounted to 0.79 percent in comparison to blue chips, which recorded only 0.47 percent. Oertmann investigated 180 stocks of small sized and large sized companies between 1985 and 1991. He identified, that small caps outperformed large stocks by 2.16 percent a year. Additionally, he recognized, that this effect arose more frequently in downward market situations. During this market period small caps outperformed large caps by 4.15 percent a year whereas in upward market periods large caps outperformed small caps. Latest academic studies, who examined the SDAX and DAX from 2001 to 2007 proved, that this effect exists, but contradicted the observation of Oertmann, who stated, that this effect arise in downward market situations. They detected an underperformance of small caps in bearish market periods and an outperformance in bullish market periods. Financial reports supported the findings of the economists and latest academic studies. During 2004 small caps recorded a yearly yield of 17 percent in comparison to blue chips, which recorded only 15.75 percent. Recent financial publications compared the development of the SDAX and the DAX from 2009 to 2010. The SDAX achieved an increase of 89 percent in comparison to the DAX, which recorded an increase of only 67 percent. Other latest financial news reported a development of 42 percent of small caps in comparison to large caps, which recorded a development of only 18 percent in 2010. Analysts forecasted the same development in 2011. Moreover, recent financial reports confirmed the observations of the academic

---

[132] Cp. Arbel, A., Strebel, P. (1982), p. 201-218; Beard, C.C., Sias, R.W. (1997), p. 19-23; Carvell, S.A., Strebel, P.J. (1987), p. 279-290; http://docs.google.com/viewer?a=v&q=cache:w7xFfEWjjcEJ: www.ftinstitutional.ca/ca/inst/en/pdf/commentary/whitepapers/white_paper_small_caps_ 081804.pdf, dated on 08.02.2011; http://docs.google.com/viewer?a=v&q=cache:yUK5aerw YcgJ:www.stern.nyu.edu/~adamodar/pdfiles/invphiloh/growthN.pdf, dated on 08.02.2011.

studies respectively that small caps outperformed in upward market situations and not in downward market situations, as Oertmann stated.[133]

Also the connection to the neglected-firm effect has been observed. Current financial news confirmed, that the development of the DAX will be observed by 40 analysts whereas the development of the SDAX will be observed only by 7 analysts.[134]

The investigations to the size effect and neglected-firm effect prove, that both effects go hand by hand. Additionally, the studies confirm, that the size effect still exists, although a size effect reversal has been observed from 1990 to 1999. Finally, the surveys demonstrate, that this is an effect, which arise in bullish market periods. However, a risk-based explanation cannot be fully confirmed.[135]

4.2.2. Other Studies to the remaining Figure Anomalies

The book-to-market-ratio anomaly has firstly been discovered by Rosenberg, Reid and Lanstein. They investigated the American stock market between 1973 and 1984 and discovered, that shares, which indicated a high book value and a low market value, i.e. value shares outperformed shares, which possessed a high market value and low book value, i.e. growth shares. Other studies of French and Fama, who investigated the same market between 1963 and 1990, confirmed the researches of the above mentioned economists. More in detail, value shares achieved a yearly yield of 24.31 percent in comparison to growth shares, which recorded a yield of only 3.7 percent a year. Similar results have been provided by O'Shaughnessy for the sample period 1951 to 1996, Lakonishok et al. for the observation period of 1968 and 1990 as well as by Damodaran, who investigated the same market from 1991 to 2001. Contrary, Schwert detected an insignificant negative yield of minus 0.20 percent from 1994 to 2002. However, economic studies

---

[133] Cp. Domke, H.M. (1987), p. 92 ff; Oertmann, P. (1994), p. 229-259; Stehle, R. (1997), p. 237-260; http://papers.ssrn.com/sol3/papers.cfm?abstract_id=952472, dated on 08.02.2011; http://www.fazfinance.net/Aktuell/Boerse-und-Anlage/Indexfonds-schlaegt-fast-alle-gemanagten-Produkte-und-ist-billiger-3966.html, dated on 08.02.2011; http://www.manager-magazin.de/finanzen/artikel/0,2828,711496,00.html, dated on 08.02.2011; http://www.welt.de/finanzen/geldanlage/article11517991/Die-zweite-Boersenliga-schlaegt-den-Dax.html, dated on 08.02.2011.

[134] Cp. http://www.tagesspiegel.de/wirtschaft/m-und-s-dax-klein-und-fein/1860836.html, dated on 08.02.2011.

[135] Cp. http://papers.ssrn.com/sol3/papers.cfm?abstract_id=952472, dated on 08.02.2011.

from Hubert Portfolio AG contradicted his findings and confirmed this effect from 1997 to 2003.[136]

This figure anomaly has been observed on international markets too. Chan et al. detected this effect on the Japanese stock market from 1971 to 1988. Capaul et al. examined the international market from 1981 to 1992 and discovered the same effect. Fama and French extended their researches also on 12 international markets and monitored a yearly outperformance of 5.6 percent from 1975 to 1995. This effect has also been discovered on the German stock market by the economist Wallmeier between 1967 and 1994. Although growth shares obtained higher yields, he detected that this has been a short-term performance. In the long-term value shares outperformed them by 12.6 percent a year. This performance on German stock markets has been reconfirmed by financial publications from 2005 and 2008. Companies like Daimler, Infineon, Münchener Rück, ThyssenKrupp and Volkswagen, which indicated a high book value respectively a book-to-market ratio lower one achieved higher yields in comparison to those, which indicated a high market value respectively a book-to-market ratio above one. Also recent reports of Allianz Global Investors confirmed a long-term outperformance of value shares in 2009.[137]

The studies concerning the book-to-market ratio effect supply the prove, that value shares outperform growth share in the long-term and that this effect still exists. However, the risk-based explanation cannot be confirmed.[138]

Another figure anomaly, which has empirically been proved is the price-earnings-ratio effect. Nicholson, was the first economist, who detected this phenomenon on the American stock market from 1939 to 1959. According to his studies, shares, which indicated a low price-earnings-ratio gained a yearly yield of 13.5 percent in comparison to those,

---

[136] Cp. Fama, E.F., French, K.R. (1993), p. 3-56; Lakonishok, J., Shleifer, A., Vishny, R.W. (1994), p. 1541-1578; Lanstein, R., Reid, K., Rosenberg, B. (1985), p. 9-16; O'Shaughnessy, J.P. (1999), p. 53 ff; Schwert, G.W. (2003), p. 939-974; http://docs.google.com/viewer?a=v&q=cache:a6L mzK1i78sJ:www.stern.nyu.edu/~adamodar/pdfiles/invphil/ch8.pdf, dated on 08.02.2011; http://docs.google.com/viewer?a=v&q=cache:geJ2RgSMd1sJ:www.antizyklisch-investieren.de/analysen/KBV-Value-Strategie_Keimling.pdf, dated on 08.02.2011.

[137] Cp. Capaul, C., Rowley, I., Sharpe, W.F. (1993), p. 27-36; Chan, L.K.C., Hamao, K., Lakonishok, J. (1991), p. 1739-1764; Fama, E.F., French, K.R. (1998), p. 1975-1999; Wallmeier, M. (2000), p. 27-57; http://www.focus.de/finanzen/boerse/aktien/deutsche-aktien-gross-und-guenstig_aid_300074.html, dated on 08.02.2011; http://docs.google.com/viewer?a=v&q=cache: 6737VAfg6l4J:www.allianzglobalinvestors.de/kapitalmarktanalyse/publikationen/PortfolioPraxis -Value-oder-Growth.pdf, dated on 08.02.2011.

[138] Cp. http://docs.google.com/viewer?a=v&q=cache:geJ2RgSMd1sJ:www.antizyklisch-investieren.de/analysen/KBV-Value-Strategie_Keimling.pdf, dated on 08.02.2011.

which indicated a high price-earnings-ratio, so called glamour shares. These shares earned a yearly yield of only 7.4 percent. Further studies of Basu et al. confirmed this observation. Between 1963 and 1977 Reinganum recognized a daily above-average yield of 0.0165 percent of low price-earnings-ratio shares and a daily negative average yield of minus 0.0124 percent of high price-earnings-ratio shares. The studies of Fama and French showed similar results. Low price-earnings-ratio shares outperformed high price-earnings-ratio shares by 10 percent a year from 1963 to 1990. Lakonishok et al. spot a yearly outperformance of 3.9 percent from 1968 to 1990. O'Shaughnessy detected a yearly outperformance of 2.96 percent of low price-earnings-ratio shares between 1951 and 1996. Damodaran expanded the studies of Fama and French and detected an outperformance of 12 percent a year from 1991 to 2001. The last economist Malkiel identified a similar performance from 1926 to 2001. Recent financial reports of Huber Portfolio AG confirmed the results of all mentioned economists and realized this effect from 1997 to 2003.[139]

Damodaran extended his examination on international markets and evidenced this anomaly based on the figures of Merrill Lynch Survey of Proprietary Indices from 1989 to 1994. This has also been done by French and Fama from 1975 to 1997. Low price-earnings-ratio shares outperformed high price-earnings-ratio shares by 4.1 percent a year. On emerging markets they outperformed by 12.8 percent a year from 1987 to 1995. Chan et al. recorded this effect on the Japanese stock market between 1971 and 1988. Shares with a low price-earnings ratio recorded a monthly yield of 1.9 percent, which was 0.4. percent points higher than those of high price-earnings ratio shares.[140] Wallmeier detected this effect on the German stock market from 1967 to 1994. Low price-earnings ratio shares outperformed glamour shares by 7.2 percent a year. Also recent financial reports of Huber Portfolio AG confirmed these results and realized this effect on international markets from 1990 to 2004.[141]

---

[139] Cp. Basu, S. (1977), p. 663-682; Campbell, J.Y., Shiller, R.J. (1988), p. 661-676; Fama, E.F., French, K.R. (1992), p. 427-465; Lakonishok, J., Shleifer, A., Vishny, R.W. (1994), p. 1541-1578; Malkiel, B.G. (2003), p. 59-82; Nicholson, S.F. (1960), p. 43-45; O'Shaughnessy, J.P. (1999), p. 53 ff; Reinganum, (1981), p. 19-46; http://docs.google.com/viewer?a=v&q=cache: 3C1OGWbfFW4J:starcapital.de/files/KGV-Value-Strategie_Keimling.pdf, dated on 08.02.2011.
[140] Cp, Chan, L.K.C., Hamao, K., Lakonishok, J. (1991), p. 1739-1764.
[141] Cp. Chan, L.K.C., Hamao, K., Lakonishok, J. (1991), p. 1739-1764; Damodaran, A. (2002), p. 138; Fama, E.F., French, K.R. (1998), p. 1975-1999; Wallmeier, M. (2000), p. 27-57. http://docs.google.com/viewer?a=v&q=cache:3C1OGWbfFW4J:starcapital.de/files/KGV-Value-Strategie_Keimling.pdf, dated on 08.02.2011.

The investigations and economic reports referring to the price-earnings-ratio effect demonstrate, that this effect still exists. However, the risk-based explanation cannot be confirmed.[142]

4.3. Empirical Evidence to the Market Efficiency Anomalies

Just like the calendar and figure anomalies there exist also several studies, which empirically evidence the existence of the market efficiency anomalies as well. In order not to extrapolate the frame of this thesis this part will concentrates only on the index effect, which will be proved on the S&P 500 followed by the bubbles and crashs, which will be demonstrated on the Tulipmania, which occurred on the Dutch stock market.

4.3.1. Index Effect evidenced on the S&P 500

As already explained in 3.3.1. this effect involves increasing yields of companies, which add an index and decreasing yields of companies, which delete an index. There were several economists, who researched this effect based on companies, which entered and left the S&P 500 between 1966 and 2008.[143]

The first economist, who identified this effect was Shleifer. He investigated the stock price reactions of companies, which entered the S&P 500 between 1966 and 1983. He detected permanent price reactions of 2.8 percent respectively the stock prices continued to increase 20 days after the effective day. This permanent index effect for index additions has been confirmed by further economists as well. Two of those were Dhillon and Johnson, who monitored this effect from 1978 to 1988. They recognized permanent price reactions of 3.33 percent. Edmister et al. detected also permanent price reactions, namely 3.27 percent between 1983 and 1989. Contrary, Beneish and Whaley discovered a permanent as well as a temporary index effect for companies, which entered the S&P 500 between 1986 and 1994. More detailed, they observed permanent price reactions of 3.67 percent from 1986 to 1988. However, between 1989 and 1994 they noticed temporary price reactions, namely stock price reactions of 3.08 percent, which arose one day after the announcement day. Further price increases of 4.1. percent has been recognized

---

[142] Cp. Daniel, K., Titman, S. (1997), p. 29.
[143] Between the sample period of 1966 and 1988 the announcement day and effective day have been the same. This has been changed. Since 1989 it exists a time period of five days.

till the effective day. However, afterwards the stock prices decreased to 2 percent.[144]

Other economists examined not only stock price reactions for index additions, but also for index deletions. Two of those were Lamoureux and Wansley, who examined the index effect between 1966 and 1985. They noticed a temporary index effect for companies, which entered, but also which left the index. Between 1966 and 1975 they detected price reactions of 5 percent for companies, which add the index. Similar results have been made from 1976 to 1985. Within this period they observed price reactions of 2.5 percent. However, the stock prices decreased 20 days after its index entry. This short-term performance has also been identified for index deletions. Those companies recorded negative price reactions of minus 1.11 percent. The temporary index effect for index entries and deletions has been confirmed by further studies of Harris and Gurel between 1973 and 1983. From 1973 to 1977 no index effect has been observed. Since 1977 they recorded above average price reactions of 3.1 percent for companies, which entered the index and negative stock price reactions of minus 1.4 percent for companies, which left the index. Contrary observations have been made by Woolridge and Ghosh between 1977 and 1983. They detected a permanent index effect for companies, which entered the S&P 500 and a temporary index effect for companies, which left this index. More detailed, they discovered price reactions of 2.77 percent for companies, which entered the index. These positive reactions still existed one month later. For companies, which left the index negative price reactions have been recorded, but which have not been as high as the positive reactions and which arose temporary. Contrary, Jain, who examined the market within the same period and Arnott and Vincent, who researched the market between 1980 and 1984 detected a permanent index effect for both – index additions and index deletions. Jain recorded above average stock price reactions of 3.07 percent for companies, which entered the index and negative stock price reactions of minus 1.16 percent for companies, which left the index. Arnott and Vincent recorded a positive price reaction of 2.71 percent, which still existed 4 weeks after its index entry. For companies, which left the index the negative reactions amounted to minus 1.92 percent. This negative performance increased to minus 12.57 percent within 19 days after the index deletion. This has been confirmed by Lynch and Mendenhall, who detected the market between 1990 and 1995. They identified positive price reactions of 3.8 per-

---

[144] Cp. Beneish, M.D., Whaley, R.E. (1996), p. 1909-1930; Dhillon, U., Johnson, H. (1991), p. 75-85; Edmister, R.O., Graham, S.A., Pirie, W.L.(1994), p. 333-346; Shleifer, A. (1986), p. 579-590.

cent for companies, which entered the index and a negative price reactions of minus 12.7 percent for companies, which left the index. The stock prices for index entries decreased to 2.1 percent. The same decrease has been observed for index deletions. Their stock prices increased to minus 5.6 percent. However, they noticed that the long-term price reactions lasted longer than the short-term price reactions.[145]

Publications from Standard & Poor's stated, that the index effect weaken. From 1998 to 2008 a decrease in price reactions from 6.05 to 3.76 percent for index entries has been noted. However, this effect doe not vanish completely, but has recently been observed by First Solar, which entered the S&P 500 in October 2009. The stock price increased to 6 percent after the announcement of its index entry. More detailed, the stock price increased from 143.70 USD to 152.6 USD. After the effective day the stock price decreased to 145 USD, which was still higher than the recorded stock price before its index entry. Same developments have been observed for companies, which left the index in 2003. Royal Dutch's stock price decreased by 7.1 percent. Unilever's stock price decreased by 6.2 percent.[146]

All economic examinations and publications regarding the index effect confirm, that this effect weaken, but still exists. The index entry of First Solar as well the index deletion of Royal Dutch and Unilever prove the temporary existence of this effect.

4.3.2. Bubbles and Crashs evidenced on the Tulipmania

The cause of the bubble on the Dutch stock market was created through the fascination in a tulip bulb originated from Turkey, which created extraordinary and unique petals, due to a virus. During this period tulips indicated prestige and were owned by more wealthy people. One of the most famous tulip, named Semper Augustus amounted to 1,000 guilder, which increased to 1,200 guilder in 1624 and to 5,000 guilder in 1633. Bulb growers noted the increased demand and hence the speculation began. During this time they have been traded on non institutional markets respectively auctions took place in pubs. Firstly they have been traded during harvest time, but due to increased demand

---

[145] Cp. Arnott, R.D., Vincent, S.J. (1986), p. 29-33; Ghosh, C., Woolridge, R.J. (1986), p. 13-24; Harris, L.E., Gurel, E. (1986), p. 815-829; Jain, P.C. (1987), p. 58-65; Lamoureux, C.G., Wansley, J.W. (1987), p. 53-69; Lynch, A.W., Mendenhall, R.R. (1997), p. 351-383.

[146] Cp. http://docs.google.com/viewer?a=v&q=cache:gLiWWmB7f30J:www2.standardandpoors.com/ spf/pdf/index/The_Shrinking_Index_Effect.pdf, dated on 08.02.2011; http://www.fazfinance.net/ Aktuell/Boerse-und-Anlage/Auslaendische-Werte-im-SAndP-500-werden-ersetzt-7929.html, dated on 08.02.2011; http://www.deraktionaer.de/aktien-usa/first-solar--kurssprung-nach-indexaufnahme-10922479.htm, dated on 08.02.2011.

the trade has been extended to the whole year, i.e. already in this stage tulip bulbs have been traded, which still have been in the ground.[147]

Since 1634 the institutional trade began and hence the bubble. In this year the stock prices of common tulip bulbs began to increase, due to access of non-professionals like butchers and weavers. The rising demand in France strengthened the demand and supply on the Dutch stock market and thus increased the stock prices and raised the speculation on tulip bulbs. Euphoria seized the market.[148]

In 1635 the stock prices increased further and speculators short-sold tulip bulbs, which they don't owned on speculators, who don't possessed the money, but purchased them, in order to short-sell them to other speculators with the aim to earn gains. During one day this non existing bulb has been traded to ten times. Trading and competition increased.[149]

In January 1637 the bubble hit one's pick. The tulip bulbs have been traded for 90,000 guilder, which corresponds to 90,000 Euro. The stock price for the famous tulip increased to 10,000 guilder. During this period professional traders – in this period wealthy people – left the stock market, but non-professionals believed in further stock price increases.[150]

In February 1637 the stock prices hit rock bottom. At an auction in Haarlem nobody was ready to buy a bulb. This destroyed the confidence, the bubble collapsed and the crash began. Panic seized the market. Due to fear of non-accomplishment of contracts it resulted in mass short-sales, which leaded to a stock price decrease of 95 percent.[151]

This bubble was not an exception. Further provided examples are the Wall Street Crash, so called black Friday in 1929 and the dot.com bubble in 1990.[152]

---

[147] Cp. Bernecker, H.A. (2008), p. 51-52; Gallander, B. (2003), p. 5; Goldgar, A. (2007), p. 2; http://www.prod.bulbsonline.org/ibc/se/publiek/information.jsf/Information/flowerbulb-history/Tulip-time-table.html, dated on 08.02.2011.
[148] Cp. Garber, P.M. (1994), p. 60; Poitras, G. (2009), p. 496.
[149] Cp. Rapp, D. (2009), p. XVI.
[150] Cp. Franke, D. (2004), p. 9; Rapp, D. (2009), p. XVII.
[151] Cp. Bender, A. (2004), p. 90; Glebe, D. (2008), p. 64.
[152] Cp. Fleckenstein, W.A., Sheehan, F. (2008), p. 39; Greenspan, S. (2009), p. 133.

5. Conclusion

5.1. Critical Acclaim

The empirical part of this thesis proved, that capital market anomalies respectively phenomena exist and that they cannot fully be explained with the classical capital market theory. Hence this theory is more and more subject to critical remarks, because it doesn't reflect the reality and thus lose confidence. This leads to the fact that the homo oeconomicus is obsolete and no longer regarded as valid and appropriate. Therefore, the once as pseudo-science regarded research proved, that the involvement of soft factors contributes to its explanation, while demonstrating, that human's irrationality leads to faulty decisions, which in turn will be reflected on the capital market and hence leads to capital market anomalies respectively phenomena.

5.2. Target Achievement

The aim of this thesis was to demonstrate how human behaviour, namely human's irrationality influences the development on the capital market respectively Behavioural Finance serves as explanation for the empirically observed capital market anomalies. The empirical evidence in chapter four supports, that capital market anomalies respectively phenomena cannot sufficiently be explained with rational respectively economical reasons. This is were Behavioural Finance comes into force, which has been demonstrated in chapter three.

5.3. Perspective

Although Behavioural Finance provides explanations for these phenomena it only gives a few hints how practical solution concepts, which consider the relevant results of Behavioural Finance, should be designed. Hence this theory has not fully been accepted, i.e. will not replace the classical capital market theory. However, this theory can be expected to become more and more relevant during the next years, which will lead to a further evolution of this non-finalized theory.

Bibliography

Akert, R.M., Aronson, E., Wilson, T.D. (2008): Sozialpsychologie, 6th ed., Munich 2008

Andrews, P.W., Haselton, M.G., Nettle, D. (2005): The Evolution of Cognitive Bias, in: Buss, D.M. (Ed.), The Handbook of Evolutionary Psychology, Hoboken 2005, p. 724-746

Anwander Phan-huy, S. (1998): Nachfrageseitige Akzeptanz von Technologien im Ernährungsbereich, in: Rieder, P. (Ed.), Diss., Zurich 1998

Arbel, A., Strebel, P. (1982): The Neglected and Small Firm Effects, in: The Financial Review, 1982, Vol. 17, No. 4, p. 201-218

Ariel, R. A. (1987): A monthly effect in stock returns, in: Journal of Financial Economics, 1987, Vol. 18, No. 1, p. 161-174

Arnold, G. (2008): Corporate Financial Management, 4th ed., Harlow 2008

Arnott, R. D., Vincent, S. J. (1986): S&P Additions and Deletions: A Market Anomaly, in: The Journal of Portfolio Management, 1986, Vol. 13, No. 1, p. 29-33

Aschoff, H. (2006): Auf der Suche nach dem heiligen Gral: Das Aktienbarometer zur Bestimmung der optimalen Investitionsquote, in: Aschoff, H. (Ed.), Die Investmentstrategien der Profis, Munich 2006, p. 27-58

Atrill, P. (2009): Financial Management for Decision Makers, 5th ed., Harlow 2009

Bak, J. (2003): Aktienrecht zwischen Markt und Staat: Eine ökonomische Kritik des Prinzips der Satzungsstrenge, in: Behrens, P., Holler, M., Ott, C., Schäfer, H.-B., Walz, R. (Eds.), Ökonomische Analyse des Rechts, Diss., Wiesbaden 2003

Baker, H.K., Nofsinger, J.R. (2010): Behavioral Finance: Investors, Corporations, and Markets, Hoboken 2010

Balaban, E. (1995): Day of the Week Effects: New Evidence from an Emerging Stock Market, in: Applied Economics Letters, 1995, Vol. 2, No. 5, p. 139-143

Banz, R.W. (1981): The Relationship Between Return and Market Value of Common Stocks, in: Journal of Financial Economics, 1981, Vol. 9, No. 1, p. 3-18

Barone, E. (1990): The Italian Stock Market: Efficiency and Calendar Anomalies, in: Journal of Banking and Finance, 1990, Vol. 14, No. 2-3, p. 483-510

Basu, S. (1977): Investment Performance of Common Stocks in Relation to their Price-Earnings Ratios: A Test of the Efficient Market Hypothesis, in: Journal of Finance; 1977, Vol. 32, No. 3, p. 663-682

Beard, C.C., Sias, R.W. (1997): Is there a Neglected-Firm Effect ?, in: Financial Analysts Journal, 1997, Vol. 53, No. 5, p. 19-23

Becker, A. (2009): Private Equity Buyout Fonds – Value Creation in Portfoliounternehmen, in: Bernet, B., Geiger, H., Grünbichler, A., Hirszowicz, C., Kilgus, E., Spremann, K., Volkart, R. (Eds.), Bank- und finanzwirtschaftliche Forschungen, Vol. 391, Diss., Berne 2009

Beckmann, J., Heckhausen, H. (2006): Situative Determinanten des Verhaltens, in: Heckhausen, J., Heckhausen, H. (Eds.), Motivation und Handeln, 3rd ed., Heidelberg 2006, p. 73-104

Behrens, B. (2010): Nachhaltiges Management und Theatralität – Inszenierung und Simulation als Instrumente der Widerspruchsbewältigung, in: Hülsmann, M., Müller-Christ, G., (Eds.), Nachhaltigkeit und Management, Vol. 6, Diss., Berlin, Münster, Zurich 2010

Bender, A. (2004): Amsterdam: City Guide, London, Melbourne, Oakland, Paris 2004

Berges, A., McConnell, J.J., Schlarbaum, G.G. (1984): An Investigation of the Turn-of-the-Year Effect, the Small Firm Effect and the Tax-Loss Selling Pressure Hypothesis in Canadian Stock Returns, in: Journal of Finance, 1984, Vol. 39, No. 1, p. 185-192

Bergold, U., Mayer, B. (2005): Markt und Meinung: Mit Behavioral Finance und Technische Analyse zu den Gewinnern gehören, 2nd ed., Munich 2005

Berndt, R. (1996): Marketing 1: Käuferverhalten, Marktforschung und Marketing-Prognosen, 3rd ed., Berlin, Heidelberg, New York 1996

Bernecker, H.A. (2008): Wie Blasen so platzen, in: Bernecker, H.A. (Ed.), Der Börsenleitfaden: Sicher agieren an den internationalen Kapitalmärkten, Munich 2008, p. 47-58

Berument, H, Kiymaz, H. (2001): The Day of the Week Effect on Stock Market Volatility, in: Journal of Economics and Finance, 2001, Vol. 25, No. 2, p. 181-193

Beneish, M.D., Whaley, R.E. (1996): An Anatomy of the "S&P Game": The Effects of Changing the Rules, in: Journal of Finance, 1996, Vol. 51, No. 5, p. 1909-1930

Beyer, S., Compton, W.S., Kunkel, R.A. (2003): The turn-of-the-month effect still lives: The international evidence, in: International Review of Financial Analysis, 2003, Vol. 12, No. 2, p. 207-221

Bitz, M., Stark, G. (2008): Finanzdienstleistungen: Darstellung, Analyse, Kritik, 8th ed., Munich 2008

Böhme, U. (2009): Investment Engineering für Online Broker: Entwicklung, effiziente Ausgestaltung und Bewertung von Transaktionsabwicklungsleistungen, in: Locarek-Junge, H., Röder, K., Wahrenburg, M. (Eds.), Finanzierung, Kapitalmarkt und Banken, Vol. 64, Diss., Lohmar – Cologne 2009

Bogun, R. (2008): Nachhaltigkeitsdiskurs, Umwelt- und Risikobewusststein: Ansatzpunkte für ein nachhaltig(er)es Konsumentenverhalten ?, in: Lange, H. (Ed.), Nachhaltigkeit als radikaler Wandel: Die Quadratur des Kreises ?, Wiesbaden 2008, p. 123-148

Bortenlänger, C., Kirstein, U. (2009): Börse für Dummies: Machen Sie mehr aus Ihrem Geld !, 2nd ed., Weinheim 2009

Bott, C. (2002): Aktionärsstruktur, Kontrolle und Erfolg von Unternehmen, in: Schmidt, H. (Ed.), Schriftenreihe des Instituts für Geld - und Kapitalverkehr der Universität Hamburg, Diss., Wiesbaden 2002

Bouchet, M.H., Clark, E., Groslambert, B. (2003): Country Risk Assessment: A Guide to Global Investment Strategy, Chichester 2003

Bousquet, L., Solnik, B. (1990): Day-of-the-week effect on the Paris Bourse, in: Journal of Banking and Finance, 1990, Vol. 14, No. 2-3, p. 461-468

Brandl, P.K. (2010): Crash-Kommunikation: Warum Piloten versagen und Manager Fehler machen, Offenbach 2010

Breuer, W., Gürtler, M., Schuhmacher, F. (2006): Portfoliomanagement II: Weiterführende Anlagestrategien, Wiesbaden 2006

Brown, P., Kleidon, A.W., Marsh, T.A. (1983): New evidence on the nature of size-related anomalies in stock prices, in: Journal of Financial Economics, 1983, Vol. 12, No. 1, p. 33-56

Brühwiler, B. (1994): Internationale Industrieversicherung: Risk Management, Unternehmungsführung, Erfolgsstrategien, Karlsruhe 1994

Burghardt, R., Werner, T. (2006): Der graue Kapitalmarkt: Chancen und Risiken, Wiesbaden 2006

Cadsby, C.B., Ratner, M. (1992): Turn-of-month and pre-holiday effects on stock returns: Some international evidence, in: Journal of Banking and Finance, 1992, Vol. 16, No. 3, p. 497-509

Campbell, J.Y., Shiller, R.J. (1988): Stock Prices, Earnings and Expected Dividends, in: Journal of Finance, 1988, Vol. 43, No. 3, p. 661-676

Capaul, C., Rowley, I., Sharpe, W.F. (1993): International Value and Growth Stock Returns, in: Financial Analysts Journal, 1993, Vol. 49, No. 1, p. 27-36

Carvell, S.A., Strebel, P.J. (1987): Is There a Neglected Firm Effect ?, in: Journal of Business Finance & Accounting, 1987, Vol. 14, No. 2, p. 279-290

Chan, L.K.C., Hamao, Y., Lakonishok, J. (1991): Fundamentals and Stock Returns in Japan, in: Journal of Finance, 1991, Vol. 46, No. 5, p. 1739-1764

Chang, E.C., Pinegar, J.M., Ravichamdram, R. (1993): International Evidence on the Robustness of the Day-of-the-Week Effect, in: Journal of Financial and Quantitative Analysis, 1993, Vol. 28, No. 4, p. 497-513

Choudhry, T. (2000): Day of the Week Effect in Emerging Asian Stock Markets: Evidence from the GARCH Model, in: Applied Financial Economics, 2000, Vol. 10, No. 3, p. 235-242

Conze, O. (2007): Kundenloyalität durch Kundenvorteile: Segmentspezifische Analyse und Implikationen für das Kundenbeziehungsmanagement, in: Roland Berger Strategy Consultants – Academic Network (Ed.), Schriften zum europäischen Management, Diss., Wiesbaden 2007

Compton, W.S., Kunkel, R.A. (1998): A Tax-Free Exploitation of the Turn-of-the-Month Effect: C.R.E.F., in: Financial Services Review, 1998, Vol. 7, No. 1, p. 11-23

Copeland, T.E., Shastri, K., Weston, J.F. (2008): Finanzierungstheorie und Unternehmenspolitik: Konzepte der Kapitalmarktorientierten Unternehmensfinanzierung, 4th ed., Munich 2008

Cross, F. (1973): The Behavior of Stock Prices on Fridays and Mondays, in: Financial Analysts Journal, 1973, Vol. 29, No. 6, p. 67-69

Crupi, V., Hartmann, S. (2010): Formal and Empirical Methods in Philosophy of Science, in: Stadler, F. (Ed.), Philosophy of Science in a European Perspective, Dordrecht, Heidelberg, London, et al. 2010, Vol. 1, p. 87-98

Damodaran, A. (2002): Investment Valuation: Tools and Techniques for Determining the Value of Any Asset, 2nd ed., New York 2002

Daniel, K., Hirshleifer, D., Subrahmanyam, A. (1998): Investor Psychology and Security Market Under- and Overreactions, in: Journal of Finance, 1998, Vol. 53, No. 6, p. 1839-1885

Daniel, K., Titman, S. (1997): Evidence on the Characteristics of Cross Sectional Variation in Stock Returns, in: Journal of Finance, 1997, Vol. 52, No. 1, p. 1-33

De Bondt, W.F.M., Thaler, R.H. (1989): Anomalies: A Mean-Reverting Walk Down Wall Street, in: Journal of Economic Perspectives, 1989, Vol. 3, No. 1, p. 189-202

Decker, M. (2009): Behavioral Finance: Anlegerverhalten erfolgreich nutzen, Hamburg 2009

Dhillon, U., Johnson, H. (1991): Changes in the Standard and Poor's 500 List, in: Journal of Business, 1991, Vol. 64, No. 1, p. 75-85

Diehl, S. (2009): Reale und mediale Produkterfahrungen: Analyse und Vergleich der Wirkungen von Experience- und Cross-Media-Marketingmaßnahmen, Series: Forschungsgruppe Konsum und Verhalten, Wiesbaden 2009

Diller, H. (2008): Preispolitik, in: Diller, H., Köhler, R. (Eds.), 4th ed., Stuttgart 2008

Domke, H.M. (1987): Rendite und Risiko von Aktien kleiner Börsengesellschaften: Eine empirische Untersuchung der Performance deutscher Nebenwerte in den Jahren 1971 bis 1980, Series: Europäische Hochschulschriften, Vol. 770, Berne, Frankfurt am Main, New York 1987

Drabe, K., Kondert, K., Lippert, T., Neusel, T., Schirp, W. (2009): Geld anlegen – aber sicher: Chancen und Risiken von Anlageformen. Ihre Rechte, wenn das Geld verloren scheint, Vienna 2009

Duggan, M. (1999): Share Markets and Psychology, in: Earl, P.E., Kemp, S. (Eds.), The Elgar Companion to Consumer Research and Economic Psychology, Cheltenham, Northampton 1999, p. 531-537

Edmister, R.O., Graham, S.A., Pirie, W.L. (1994): Excess Returns of Index Replacement Stocks: Evidence of Liquidity and Substitutability, in: Journal of Financial Research, 1994, Vol. 17, No. 3, p. 333-346

Egloff, B. (2002): Praktikum und Studium: Diplom-Pädagogik und Humanmedizin zwischen Studium, Beruf, Biographie und Lebenswelt, Series: Studien zur Erziehungswissenschaft und Bildungsforschung, Vol. 20, Opladen 2002

Faith, C.M. (2007): Die Strategien der Turtle Trader: Geheime Methoden, die gewöhnliche Menschen in legendäre Trader verwandeln, 2nd ed., Munich 2007

Fama, E.F., French, K.R. (1992): The Cross-Section of Expected Stock Returns, in: Journal of Finance, 1992, Vol. 47, No. 2, p. 427-465

Fama, E.F., French, K.R. (1993): Common risk factors in the returns on stocks and bonds, in: Journal of Financial Economics, 1993, Vol. 33, No. 1, p. 3-56

Fama, E.F., French, K.R. (1998): Value versus Growth: The International Evidence, in: Journal of Finance, 1998, Vol. 53, No. 6, p. 1975-1999

Fan, X.M., Groenewold, N., Tang, S.H.K., Wu, Y. (2004): Empirical studies: a survey, in: Groenewold, N. (Ed.), The Chinese Stock Market: Efficiency, Predictability and Profitability, Series: Advances in Chinese Economic Studies, Cheltenham, Northampton 2004, p. 44-72

Felser, G. (2010): Wahrnehmung von Preisen und Kosten aus psychologischer Sicht, in: Fischer, M.G., Meyer, S. (Eds.), Gesundheit und Wirtschaftswachstum: Recht, Ökonomie und Ethik als Innovationsmotoren für die Medizin, Berlin, Heidelberg, Dordrecht, et al. 2010, p. 193-204

Fiala, J., Merten, H.-L. (2008): Wer hat unser Geld verbrannt ? Vermögen absichern – Risiken vermeiden, Finanzwissen für Anleger und Berater, Regensburg 2008

Fields, M.J. (1931): Stock Prices: A Problem in Verification, in: Journal of Business of the University of Chicago, 1931, Vol. 4, p. 415

Fieseler, C. (2008): Die Kommunikation von Nachhaltigkeit: Gesellschaftliche Verantwortung als Inhalt der Kapitalmarktkommunikation, Wiesbaden 2008

Fleckenstein, W.A., Sheehan, F. (2008): Mr. Bubble: Wie Alan Greenspan die Welt an den Abgrund führte, Munich 2008

Florissen, A. (2005): Preiscontrolling: Rationalitätssicherung im Preismanagement, in: Weber, J. (Ed.), Schriften des Center for Controlling & Management (CCM), Vol. 17, Diss., Wiesbaden 2005

Franke, D. (2004): Die Dynamik des Crashs – Spektakuläre Wirtschafts- und Finanzkrisen, in: Die Bank, 2004, No. 8, p. 8-13

French K.R. (1980): Stock return and the weekend effect, in: Journal of Financial Economics, 1980, Vol. 8, No. 1, p. 55-69

Friebel, M. (2010): Die Welt der Börsenindizes: Marktbarometer und intelligente Anlageklassen, Hamburg 2010

Gallander, B. (2003): The Contrarian Investor's Thirteen: How to Earn Superior Returns in the Stockmarket, Toronto, 2003

Garber, P.M. (1994): Tulipmania, in: Flood, R.P., Garber, P.M., (Eds.), Speculative Bubbles, Speculative Attacks, and Policy Switching, Massachusetts 1994, p. 55-82

Geier, C. (2009): Zeitvariable Risikoprämien als Erklärung für Marktanomalien, 2nd ed., Hamburg 2009

Gibbons, M.R., Hess, P. (1981): Day of the Week Effects and Asset Returns, in: Journal of Business, 1981, Vol. 54, No. 4, p. 579-596

Glebe, D. (2008): Die globale Finanzkrise: Alle Informationen zur Wirtschaftskrise 2007-2009, dazu Geschichte und umfassendes Gesamtwissen zu den bisherigen Finanzkrisen dieser Welt. Ursachen, Auswirkungen, Reaktionen, Series: Börse verstehen, Norderstedt 2008

Globocnik, D. (2011): Front End Decision Making: Das Entstehen hochgradig neuer Innovationsvorhaben in Unternehmen, in: Gemünden, H.G., Leker, J., Salomo, S., Schewe, G., Talke, K. (Eds.), Betriebswirtschaftliche Studien in forschungsintensiven Industrien, Wiesbaden 2011

Götte, R. (2001): Aktienanleihen, Discount-Zertifikate, Fonds, Genußscheine: Risiken und Strategien, Marburg 2001

Goldberg, J., Nitzsch, R. (2004): Behavioral Finance: Gewinnen mit Kompetenz, 4th ed., Munich 2004

Goldgar, A. (2007): Tulipmania: Money, Honor, and Knowledge in the Dutch Golden Age, Chicago, London 2007

Ghosh, C., Woolridge, R.J. (1986): Institutional Trading and Security Prices: The Case of Changes in the Composition of the S&P 500 Index, in: Journal of Financial Research, 1986, Vol. 9, No. 8, p. 13-24

Grauwe, P., Grimaldi, M. (2006): The Exchange Rate in a Behavioral Finance Framework, Princeton, Woodstock 2006

Greenspan, S. (2009): Annals of Gullibility: Why We Get Duped and How to Avoid it, Westport 2009

Greiner, M. (2008): Verhaltenstheorie: Behavioral Real Estate, in: Schulte, K.-W. (Ed.), Immobilienökonomie: Volkswirtschaftliche Grundlagen, Vol. 4, Munich 2008

Grunenberg, H., Heinrichs, H. (2009): Klimawandel und Gesellschaft: Perspektive Adaptionskommunikation, Wiesbaden 2009

Gruß, C.M.F. (2008): Revenue-Management in der Automobilindustrie: Vorgehenskonzept zur online Neuwagendistribution und Produktharmonisierung, in: Specht, D. (Ed.), Beiträge zur Produktionswirtschaft, Wiesbaden 2008

Günther, A., Haubl, R., Meyer, P., Stengel, M., Wüstner, K. (1998): Sozialwissenschaftliche Ökologie: Eine Einführung, Berlin, Heidelberg, New York 1998

Gürtler, M. Hartmann, N. (2005): Gründungsfinanzierung und beschränkte Rationalität, in: Börner, C.J., Grichnik, D. (Eds.), Entrepreneurial Finance: Kompendium der Gründungs- und Wachstumsfinanzierung, Heidelberg 2005, p. 369-390

Gultekin, M.N., Gultekin, N.B. (1983): Stock Market Seasonality: International Evidence, in: Journal of Financial Economics, 1983, Vol. 12, No. 4, p. 469-481

Guo, Z. (2002): Behavioral Finance: Die empirische Überprüfbarkeit behavioraler Modelle, Diss., St. Gallen 2002

Haas, A., Scheufele, B. (2008): Medien und Aktien: Theoretische und empirische Modellierung der Rolle der Berichterstattung für das Börsengeschehen, Wiesbaden 2008

Hadani, E.I., Holtfort, T. (2009): Technische Handelssysteme – Optimierung mittels der Ansätze der Behavioral Finance, in: Finanz Betrieb, 2009, Vol.10, p. 568-574

Häcker, J. (2009): Welche Auswirkungen hat die Finanzkrise auf das Fach "Internationale Finanzen" ?, in: Dillerup, R.; Haberlandt, K., Vogler, G. (Eds.), Heilbronner Beiträge zur Unternehmensführung: 40 Jahre Erfolgsgeschichten, Munich 2009, p. 81-96

Harris, L.E., Gurel, E. (1986): Price and Volume Effects Associated with Changes in the S&P 500 List: New Evidence for the Existence of Price Pressures, in: Journal of Finance, 1986, Vol. 41, No. 4, p. 815-829

Hauber, R. (2002): Performance Measurement in der Forschung und Entwicklung: Konzeption und Methodik, in: Bellmann, K. (Ed.), Forum Produktionswirtschaftliche Forschung, Wiesbaden 2002

Haug, M., Hirschey, M. (2006): The January Effect, in: Financial Analysts Journal, 2006, Vol. 62, No. 5, p. 78-88

Haugen, R., Lakonishok, J (1987): The Incredible January Effect, The Stock Market's Unsolved Mystery, Homewood 1987

Hauser, S.E. (2003): Informationsverarbeitung am Neuen Markt: Eine empirische Analyse der Determinanten von Kursreaktionen auf Ad-hoc-Meldungen, Diss., Wiesbaden 2003

Hausmann, C. (2009): Psychologie und Kommunikation für Pflegeberufe, 2nd ed., Vienna 2009

Heckmann, T. (2009): Markttechnische Handelssysteme, quantitative Kursmuster und saisonale Kursanomalien, in: Locarek-Junge, H., Röder, K., Wahrenburg, M. (Eds.), Finanzierung, Kapitalmarkt und Banken, Vol. 65, Diss., Lohmar – Cologne 2009

Hermann, A. (2007): Bausteine der Politik: Eine Einführung, Wiesbaden 2007

Heun, M. (2007): Finanzmarktsimulation mit Multiagentensystemen: Entwicklung eines methodischen Frameworks, Diss., Wiesbaden 2007

Himmelreich, A. (2006): Wettbewerbsvorteile in Kapitalmärkten durch softwaregestützte Handelsstrategien, Diss., Kassel 2006

Hirsch, B. (2007): Controlling und Entscheidungen, Series: Die Einheit der Gesellschaftswissenschaften, Vol. 139, Tübingen 2007

Hofmann-Unger, K., Unger, C. (2007): Yoga und Psychologie: Persönliches Wachstum und Risiken auf dem Übungsweg. Ein Leitfaden für Übende und Lehrende, 3rd ed., Ahrensburg 2007

Holtfort, T. (2009): Einfluss von Saisonalität auf den Momentumeffekt: Eine empirische Untersuchung des deutschen Aktienmarktes, Diss., Lohmar – Cologne 2009

Holtfort, T., Nelles, M., Uzik, M. (2007): Rollierende Momentum-Strategien am deutschen Aktienmarkt, in: Finanz Betrieb, 2007, Vol. 9, No. 7-8, p. 444-449

Hoose, A. (2006): Erfolgreich auf anderen Wegen: Gegen den Trend zum Börsenerfolg, in: Aschoff, H. (Ed.), Die Investmentstrategien der Profis, Munich 2006, p. 255-354

Horne, J.C., Wachowicz, J.M. (2005): Fundamentals of Financial Management, 12th ed., Harlow 2005

Hornung, R., Lächler, J. (2006): Psychologisches und soziologisches Grundwissen für Gesundheits – und Krankenpflegeberufe, 9th ed., Basel, Weinheim 2006

Jaffe, J.F., Westerfield, R. (1985): The Week-End Effect in Common Stock Returns: The International Evidence, in: Journal of Finance, 1985, Vol. 40, No. 2, p. 433-454

Jaffe, J.F., Westerfield, R. (1989): Is there a monthly effect in stock market returns ? Evidence from foreign countries, in: Journal of Banking and Finance, 1989, Vol. 13, No. 2, p. 237-244

Jain, P.C. (1987): The Effect on Stock Price of Inclusion in or Exclusion from the S&P 500, in: Financial Analysts Journal, 1987, Vol. 43, No. 1, p. 58-65

Jedrowiak, J. (2008): Die Wahl der Preislagen durch Konsumenten, in: Müller-Hagedorn, L. (Ed.), Schriften zur Handelsforschung, Vol. 101, Diss., Berlin, Cologne, Kohlhammer et al. 2008

Jeske, K.-J. (2008): Risikoentscheidungsverhalten von Führungskräften – eine empirische Untersuchung in der deutschen Versicherungswirtschaft, in: Schwebler, R., Werner, U. (Eds.), Karlsruher Reihe II, Risikoforschung und Versicherungsmanagement, Vol. 6, Diss., Karlsruhe 2008

Jörg Perrin, P. (2007): Geschlechts- und ausbildungsspezifische Unterschiede im Investitionsverhalten, in: Kühn, R., Thom, N. (Eds.), Berner Betriebswirtschaftliche Schriften, Vol. 39, Diss., Berne 2007

Jones, R.C. (1998): The Active versus Passive Debate: Perspectives of an Active Quant, in: Fabozzi, F.J. (Ed.), Selected Topics in Equity Portfolio Management, New Hope 1998, p. 67-86

Jost; P.-J. (2008): Organisation und Motivation: Eine ökonomisch-psychologische Einführung, 2nd ed., Wiesbaden 2008

Junge, P. (2010): BWL für Ingenieure: Grundlagen – Fallbeispiele – Übungsaufgaben, Wiesbaden 2010

Kahneman, D., Tversky, A. (1981): The Framing of Decisions and the Psychology of Choice, in: Science, New Series, 1981, Vol. 211, No. 4481, p. 453-458

Kamara, A. (1997): New Evidence on the Monday Seasonal in Stock Returns, in: Journal of Business; 1997, Vol. 70, No. 1, p. 63-84

Kato, K., Schallheim, J. S. (1985): Seasonal and Size Anomalies in the Japanese Stock Market, in: Journal of Financial and Quantitative Analysis, 1985, Vol. 20, No. 2, p.243-260

Keim, D. B. (1983): Size-related anomalies and stock return seasonality: Further empirical evidence, in: Journal of Financial Economics, 1983, Vol. 12, No. 1, p. 13-32

Keim, D.B., Stambaugh, R.F. (1984): A Further Investigation of the Weekend Effect in Stock Returns, in: Journal of Finance, 1984, Vol. 39, No. 3, p. 819-835

Kiehling, H. (2001): Börsenpsychologie und Behavioral Finance: Wahrnehmung und Verhalten am Aktienmarkt, Munich 2001

Kiell, G., Moerschen, T. (2003): Psychologische Determinanten von Kurs "Anomalien" am deutschen Aktienmarkt: Eine empirisch-psychologische Untersuchung auf Markoebene, in: Fischer, L. (Ed.), Wirtschaftspsychologie, Finanzpsychologie II, 2003, Vol. 5, No. 4, p. 86-100

Kiser, R. (2010): Beyond Right and Wrong: The Power of Effective Decision Making for Attorneys and Clients, Berlin, Heidelberg, London et al. 2010

70

Kitzmann, A. (2009): Massenpsychologie und Börse: So bestimmen Erwartungen und Gefühle Kursverläufe, Wiesbaden 2009

König, W. (2010): Autocrash und Kernkraft-Gau, in: Bohlender, M., Meurer, S., Münkler, H. (Eds.), Sicherheit und Risiko: Über den Umgang mit Gefahr im 21. Jahrhundert, Series: Sozialtheorie, Bielefeld 2010, p. 207-219

Kogan, P. (2009): Marktanomalien bei IPOs: Frankfurter Freiverkehr und Londoner Alternative Investment Market, Hamburg 2009

Koh, S.-K., Wong, K.A. (2000): Anomalies in Asian emerging stock markets, in: Keim, D.B., Ziemba, W.T. (Eds.), Security Market Imperfections in World Wide Equity Markets, Cambridge, Melbourne, New York 2000, p. 433-457

Kommer, G. (2001): Weltweit investieren mit Fonds: Wie Sie Ihre Gewinne erhöhen und Ihr Risiko senken können, Frankfurt am Main 2001

Kontrec-Goedecke, M. (2010): Erklärungsansätze für Performance-Persistenz bei Investmentfonds: Ein Überblick, Hamburg 2010

Kottke, N. (2005): Entscheidungs- und Anlageverhalten von Privatinvestoren: Psychologische Aspekte der Wertpapieranlage, Diss., Wiesbaden 2005

Kowalewski, J. (2008): Das Vorerwerbsrecht der Mutteraktionäre beim Börsengang einer Tochtergesellschaft: Anlegeraktionärsschutz im Konzern zwischen Neoklassik und Behavioral Finance – eine juristische und ökonomische Analyse, Diss., Tübingen 2008

Krämer; W., Runde, R. (1997): Stocks and the Weather: An Exercise in Data Mining or Yet Another Capital Market Anomaly ?, in: Empirical Economics, 1997, Vol. 22, No. 4, p. 637-641

Külpmann, M. (2004): Irrational Exuberance Reconsidered: The Cross Section of Stock Returns, 2nd ed., Series: Springer Finance, Berlin, Heidelberg, New York 2004

Lakonishok, J., Shleifer, A., Vishny, R.W. (1994): Contrarian Investment, Extrapolation, and Risk, in: Journal of Finance, 1994, Vol. 49, No. 5, p. 1541-1578

Lakonishok, J., Smidt, S. (1988): Are Seasonal Anomalies Real ? A Ninety-Year Perspective, 1988, Vol. 1, No. 4, p. 403-425

Lamoureux, C.G., Wansley, J.W. (1987): Market Effects of Changes in the Standard & Poor's 500 Index, in: Financial Review, 1987, Vol. 22, No. 1, p. 53-69

Langer, T. (1999): Alternative Entscheidungskonzepte in der Banktheorie, Series: Wirtschaftswissenschaftliche Beiträge, Vol. 170, Heidelberg 1999

Lanstein, R., Reid, K., Rosenberg, B. (1985): Persuasive evidence of market ineffi-
ciency, in: Journal of Portfolio Management, 1985, Vol. 11, No. 3, p. 9-16

Lee, C.M.C., Shleifer, A., Thaler, R.H. (1991): Investor Sentiment and the Closed-
End-Fund-Puzzle, in: Journal of Finance, 1991, Vol. 46, No. 1, p. 75-109

Lehment, T., Krumbach-Mollenhauer, P. (2007): Führen mit Psychologie: Die Ma-
nagementpraxis fest im Griff, Weinheim 2007

Levinson, M. (2010): Guide to Financial Markets, 5th ed., New York 2010

Liano, K., Lindley, J., Slater, S. (2004): The Strength of the Tax Effect at the Turn of
the Year, Department of Economics and Finance, Working Papers No 6, Mississippi
State University 2004

Liekweg, A. (2003): Risikomanagement und Rationalität: Präskriptive Theorie und
praktische Ausgestaltung von Risikomanagement, in: Weber, J. (Ed.), Schriften des
Center for Controlling & Management (CCM), Vol. 11, Diss., Wiesbaden 2003

Lies, J.J. (2003): Wandel begreifen: Die Rolle von Macht und Sozialkapital im Chan-
ge-Management, Diss., Wiesbaden 2003

Lindenmeier, J., Tscheulin, D.K: (2009): Der Einfluss verhaltenswissenschaftlicher
Aspekte in den Wirtschaftswissenschaften, in: Schüpbach, H., Tscheulin, D.K. (Eds.),
Verhaltenswissenschaftliche Grundlagen in ökonomischen Systemen, Berlin 2009, p.
11-28

Lisbach, B., Zacharopoulos, M. (2007): Gesundheitsbewusstes Verhalten fördern:
Psychologisches Basiswissen für Physio-, Sport- und Ergotherapeuten, Munich 2007

Lüscher-Marty, M. (2008): Theorie und Praxis der Geldanlage 1: Grundlagen und Ba-
sisprodukte, 2nd ed., Zurich 2008

Lupert, P. (2010): Wie werden Kosten-Nutzen-Assoziationen durch produktspezifische
Faktoren beeinflusst ? Eine Feldstudie, Vienna 2010

Lynch, A.W., Mendenhall, R.R. (1997): New Evidence on Stock Price Effects Associated with Changes in the S&P 500 Index, in: Journal of Business, 1997, Vol. 70, No. 3,
p. 351-383

Ma, S. (2004): The Efficiency of China's Stock Market, Series: The Chinese Trade and
Industry, Aldershot, Burlington 2004

Malkiel, B.G. (2003): The Efficient Market Hypothesis and Its Critics, in: Journal of
Economic Perspectives, 2003, Vol. 17, No. 1, p. 59-82

Markellos, R.N., Mills, T.C. (2008): The Econometric Modelling of Financial Time Series, 3rd ed., Cambridge, Melbourne, New York, et al. 2008

Martikainen, T., Perttunen, J., Ziemba, W.T. (1994): The turn-of-the-month effect in the world's stock markets, January 1988 – January 1990, in: Financial Markets and Portfolio Management, 1994, Vol. 8, Vol. 4., p. 41-49

McConnell, J.J., Xu, W. (2008): Equity Returns at the Turn of the Month, in: Financial Analysts Journal, 2008, Vol. 64, No. 2, p. 49-64

Mehl, F. (2001): Komplexe Bewertungen: Zur ethischen Grundlegung der Technikbewertung, Series: Technikphilosophie, Vol. 4, Münster 2001

Meyers, D.G. (2008): Psychologie, 2nd ed., Heidelberg 2008

Michelis, D. (2009): Interaktive Großbildschirme im öffentlichen Raum: Nutzungsmotive und Gestaltungsregeln, Diss., Wiesbaden 2009

Mieth, D. (2004): Aggression und Vorurteil – Die Sozialpsychologischen Bedingungen des Rassismus in sozialethischer Sicht, in: Thiel, M.-J. (Ed.), Europa, Religion und Kultur angesichts des Rassismus / Europe, spiritualites et culture face au racisme, Series: Forum Religion & Sozialkultur – Abt. A: Religions- und Kirchensoziologische Texte, Münster 2004, Vol. 11, p. 87-95

Mitchell, J.D., Ong, L.L. (2006): Seasonalities in China's Stock Markets: Cultural or Structural ?, International Monetary Fund, Working Paper 96/4, p. 1-44

Montassér, R.D. (2003): Die Rolle des Volumens bei der Aktienprognose unter besonderer Berücksichtigung der AVAS-Transformation, Series: Hallesche Schriften zur Betriebswirtschaft, Diss., Wiesbaden 2003

Moosa, I.A. (2007): The Vanishing January Effect, in: International Research Journal of Finance and Economics, 2007, No. 7, p. 92-103

Müller, M. (2008): Ich mach Geld und nicht den Abwasch: Wie Frauen zu einem kleinen Vermögen kommen, Hanover 2008

Müller-Reichart, M. (1994): Empirische und theoretische Fundierung eines innovativen Risiko-Beratungskonzeptes der Versicherungswirtschaft, Series: Passauer Reihe, Vol. 2, Diss., Karlsruhe 1994

Nicholson, S.F. (1960): Price-Earnings-Ratio, in: Financial Analysts Journal, 1960, Vol. 16, p. 43-45

Nitzsch, R. (2006): Entscheidungslehre, 3rd ed., Aachen 2006

Nitzsch, R., Stolz, O. (2006): Risikobewusst Investieren: Der Schlüssel zum kontrollierten Portfoliomanagement, Munich 2006

Noack, D. (2008): Behavioral Risk Management: Ein verhaltenswissenschaftliches Fundament für das individuelle und unternehmerische Risikomanagement, Hamburg 2008

Nolte, D. (2009): Hedge-Fonds im Portfolio von Privatinvestoren: Konsequenzen für die Anlageberatung, Diss., Lohmar – Cologne 2009

North, K. (2005): Wissensorientierte Unternehmensführung: Wertschöpfung durch Wissen, 4th ed., Wiesbaden 2005

O´Shaughnessy, J.P. (1999): Die besten Anlagestrategien aller Zeiten: Die richtigen Analyseinstrumente, Fundierter Kauf und Verkaufsentscheidungen, Überdurchschnittliche Erträge, 2nd ed., Rosenheim 1999

Oetken, P. (2010): Die deutschen Small Caps: Definition, Situation und Finanzkommunikation, Hamburg 2010

Oertmann, P. (1994): Firm-Size-Effekt am deutschen Aktienmarkt. Eine empirische Untersuchung, in: Schmalenbachs Zeitschrift für betriebswirtschaftliche Forschung, 1994, Vol. 46, No. 3, p. 229-259

Ogden, J. P. (1990): Turn-of-Month Evaluations of Liquid Profits and Stock Returns: A Common Explanation for the Monthly and January Effects, in: Journal of Finance, 1990, Vol. 45, No.4, p. 1259-1272

Parness, M. (2006): Der Weg zum Profi Trader: Dynamisch traden – Dynamisch leben, Munich 2006

Pepels, W. (2007): Segmentierungsdeterminanten im Käuferverhalten, in: Pepels, W. (Ed.), Marktsegmentierung: Erfolgsnischen finden und besetzen, 2nd ed., Düsseldorf 2007, p. 75-108

Perloff, R.M. (2003): The Dynamics of Persuasion: Communication and Attitudes in the 21st Century, 2nd ed., New Jersey 2003

Petermann, T., Revermann, C., Scherz, C. (2006): Zukunftstrends im Tourismus, Berlin 2006

Pfirsching, F. (2007): Portfoliotransaktionen von Selbstnutzern: Eine immobilienwirtschaftliche Analyse, Diss., Wiesbaden 2007

Piwinger, M. (2009): IR als Kommunikationsdisziplin, in: Kirchhoff, K.R., Piwinger, M. (Eds.), Praxishandbuch Investor Relations: Das Standardwerk der Finanzkommunikation, 2nd ed., Wiesbaden 2009, p. 13-34

Poitras, G. (2009): The Early History of Option Contracts, in: Hafner, W., Zimmermann, H. (Eds.), Vinzenz Bronzin's Option Pricing Models: Exposition and Appraisal, Berlin, Heidelberg 2009, p. 487-518

Pradhuman, S.D. (2000): Small-Cap Dynamics: Insights, Analysis, And Models, Princeton 2000

Raab, G. (2006): Ist der Homo oeconomicus noch zu retten ? Das Bild vom Menschen in der Behavioral Finance, in: Kufeld, K., Nell, V. (Eds.), Homo oeconomicus: Ein neues Leitbild in der globalisierten Welt ?, Berlin, Münster 2006

Raab, G., Unger, F. (2005): Marktpsychologie: Grundlagen und Anwendung, Series: Gabler Lehrbuch, 2nd ed., Wiesbaden 2005

Rapp, D. (2009): Bubbles, Booms, and Busts: The Rise and Fall of Financial Assets, New York 2009

Redhead, K. (2008): Personal Finance and Investments: A Behavioral Finance Perspective, Abingdon, New York 2008

Reimann, M. (2005): Modellierung von Investorenverhalten: Implikationen für interkulturelles Investor Marketing und Investor Relations, in: Enke, M. (Ed.), Integratives Marketing – Wissenstransfer zwischen Theorie und Praxis, Diss., Wiesbaden 2005

Reinganum, M.R. (1981): Misspecification of capital asset pricing: Empirical anomalies based on earnings' yields and market values, in: Journal of Financial Economics, 1981, Vol. 9, No. 1, p. 19-46

Reinganum, M.R. (1982): A Direct Test of Roll's Conjecture on the Firm Size Effect, in: Journal of Finance, 1982, Vol. 37, No.1, p. 27-35

Reinganum, M.R. (1983): The anomalous stock market behaviour of small firms in January: Empirical tests for tax-loss selling effects, in: Journal of Financial Economics, 1983, Vol. 12, No. 1, p. 89-104

Rendon, J., Ziemba, W. (2007): Is the January Effect Still Alive in the Futures Markets ?, in: Financial Markets and Portfolio Management, 2007, Vol. 21, No. 3, p. 381-396

Riesenhuber, M. (2006): Die Fehlentscheidung: Ursachen und Eskalation, in: Becker, W., Weber, J. (Eds.), Unternehmensführung & Controlling, Diss., Wiesbaden 2006

Ritter, J.R. (1988): The Buying and Selling Behavior of Individual Investors at the Turn of the Year, in: The Journal of Finance, 1988, Vol. 43, No. 3, p. 701-717

Röder, K. (1994): Gibt es den Turn-of-the-Month Effekt ? Eine empirische Analyse des deutschen Marktes von 1960 bis 1992, in: Finanzmarkt und Portfolio Management, 1994, Vol. 8, No. 4, p. 535-545

Rogalski, R.J. (1984): New Findings Regarding Day-of-the-Week Returns over Trading and Non-trading Periods: A Note, in: Journal of Finance, 1984, Vol. 39, No. 5, p. 1603-1614

Roll, R. (1981): A Possible Explanation of the Small Firm Effect, in: Journal of Finance, 1981, Vol. 36, No. 4, p. 879-888

Romppel, A. (2006): Competitive Intelligence: Konkurrenzanalyse als Navigationssystem im Wettbewerb, Berlin 2006

Rozeff, M.S. and Kinney, W.R. (1976): Capital Market Seasonality: The Case of Stock Returns, in: Journal of Financial Economics, 1976, Vol. 3, No. 4, p. 379-402

Rudolph, B. (2006): Unternehmensfinanzierung und Kapitalmarkt, Tübingen 2006

Rutkowski, L. (2008): Computional Intelligence: Methods and Techniques, Series: Neue ökonomische Grundrisse, Berlin 2008

Ryland, P. (2009): Essential Investment: An A-Z Guide, 2nd ed., New York 2009

Schmeisser, W. (2010): Corporate Finance und Risk-Management, Munich 2010

Schmidt, K. (2009): IT-Risikomanagement, in: Tiemayer, E. (Ed.), Handbuch IT-Management: Konzepte, Methoden, Lösungen und Arbeitshilfen für die Praxis, 3rd ed., Munich 2009

Schmidt-Tank, S. (2005): Indexeffekte am europäischen Kapitalmarkt: Eine Analyse aus der Perspektive börsennotierter Unternehmen, Diss., Wiesbaden 2005

Schmies, C. (2007): Behavioral Finance und Finanzmarkregulierung, in: Engel, C., Englerth, M., Lüdemann, J., Spiecker, I.. (Eds.), Recht und Verhalten: Beiträge zu Behavioral Law and Economics, Tübingen 2007, p. 165-188

Schön, M. (2006): Das Erste – kompakt: Medizinische Psychologie und Soziologie: GK1, in: Priewe, J., Tümmers, D. (Eds.), Berlin 2006

Schütz, H., Wiedemann, P.M. (2005): Was sollte ein Risikomanager über die Risikowahrnehmung wissen ?, in: Glaeßer, D., Pechlaner, H. (Eds.), Risiko und Gefahr im Tourismus: Erfolgreicher Umgang mit Krisen und Strukturbrüchen, Series: Schriften zum Tourismus und Freizeit, Berlin 2005, Vol. 4, p. 75-90

Schünemann, H. (2000): Mythos und Profit: Zur Vermittlung sozialer Interaktionsmodelle über fiktionale Informationsdienstleistungen am Beispiel des amerikanischen Bestseller-Romans, Würzburg 2000

Schwarz, N. (1997): Urteilsheuristiken und Entscheidungsverhalten, in: Frey, D., Greif, S. (Eds.), Sozialpsychologie: Ein Handbuch in Schlüsselbegriffen, 4th ed., Weinheim 1997

Schweiger, W. (2007): Theorien der Mediennutzung: Eine Einführung, Series: Studienbücher zur Kommunikations- und Medienwissenschaft, Wiesbaden 2007

Schwert G.W. (1983): Size and stock returns, and other empirical regularities, in: Journal of Financial Economics, 1983, Vol. 12, No. 1, p. 3-12

Schwert, G. W. (2003): Anomalies and market efficiency, in: Constantinides G.M., Harris, M., Stulz, R.M. (Eds.), Handbook of the Economics of Finance, 2003, Vol. 1, No. 1, Chapter 15, p. 939-974

Sewell, M. (2011): The Evolution of Entrepreneurs and Venture Capitalists, in: Yazdipour, R. (Ed.), Advances in Entrepreneurial Finance: With Applications from Behavioral Finance and Economics, Dordrecht, Heidelberg, London, et al. 2011

Shiller, R. J. (1998): Human Behavior and the Efficiency of the Financial System, in: Cowles Foundation Discussion Papers, 1998, No. 1172, p. 1-34

Shleifer, A. (1986): Do Demand Curves for Stocks Slope Down ?, in: Journal of Finance, 1986, Vol. 41, No. 3, p. 579-590

Siegel, J.J. (2008): Stocks for the Long Run: The Definitive Guide to Financial Market Returns and Long-term Investment Strategies, 4th ed., New York 2008

Spremann, K. (2006): Portfoliomanagement, Series: International Managment and Finance, 3rd ed., Munich 2006

Stanzel, M. (2007): Qualität des Aktienresearch von Finanzanalysten: Eine theoretische und empirische Untersuchung der Gewinnprognosen und Aktienempfehlungen am deutschen Kapitalmarkt, in: Bessler, W. (Ed.), Geld – Banken – Börsen, Diss., Wiesbaden 2007

Stark, G. (2005): Grundsätze zur Privatfinanz, Series: Lehr- und Handbücher zu Geld, Börse und Versicherung, Munich 2005

Steeley, J.M. (2001): A note on information seasonality and the disappearance of the weekend effect in the UK stock market, in: Journal of Banking and Finance, 2001, Vol. 25, No. 10, p. 1941-1956

Stehle, R. (1997): Der Size-Effekt am deutschen Aktienmarkt, in: Zeitschrift für Bankrecht und Bankwirtschaft, 1997, Vol. 9, No. 3, p. 237-260

Steul, M. (2003): Risikoverhalten privater Kapitalanleger: Implikationen für das Finanzdienstleistungsmarketing, Diss., Wiesbaden 2003

Strohmeier, G. (2007): Ganzheitliches Risikomanagement in Industriebetrieben: Grundlagen, Gestaltungsmodell und praktische Anwendung, in: Bauer, U., Biedermann, H., Wohinz, J.W. (Eds.), Techno-ökonomische Forschung und Praxis, Wiesbaden 2007

Thaler, R.H. (1987): Anomalies: Seasonal Movements in Security Prices II: Weekend, Holiday, Turn of the Month and Intraday Effects, in: Journal of Economic Perspectives, 1987, Vol. 1, No. 2, p. 167-177

Thaler, R.H. (1993): Advances in Behavioral Finance, in: Thaler, R.H. (Ed.), New York 1993

Theurillat, M.J. (1996): Der Schweizer Aktienmarkt: Eine empirische Untersuchung im Lichte der neueren Effizienzmarkt-Diskussion, Series: Wirtschaftliche Beiträge, Vol. 127, Heidelberg 1996

Tiggelaar, B. (2010): Träumen, Wagen, Tun: Wie Sie den schwierigsten Menschen der Welt managen: sich selbst, Offenbach 2010

Titzkus, T. (2005): Reaktive Preispolitik in industriellen Kundenbeziehungen: Eine Prozessorientierte Entscheidungshilfe zur Preisfindung auf der Grundlage subjektiver Expertenschätzungen, Diss., Wiesbaden 2005

Unger, A., Unger, F., Raab, G. (2010): Marktpsychologie: Grundlagen und Anwendung, Series: Gabler Lehrbuach, 3rd ed., Wiesbaden 2010

Völker, R. (2008): Managementkonzepte beurteilen und richtig anwenden, Munich 2008

Voigt, S. (2008): Behavioral Finance: Psychologische Erklärungsansätze für typisches Anlegerverhalten, Series: Diplomarbeit, Hamburg 2008

Vogt, G. (2009): Faszinierende Mirkoökonomie: Erlebnisorientierte Einführung, 3rd ed., Munich 2009

Wachtel, S.B. (1942): Certain Observation on Seasonal Movements in Stock Prices, in: Journal of Business of the University of Chicago, 1942, Vol. 15, No. 2, p. 184-193

Wärneryd, K.E. (2001): Stock-Market Psychology: How people value and trade stocks, Cheltenham, Northampton 2001

Wahren, H.-K. (2009): Anlegerpsychologie, Wiesbaden 2009

Wallmeier, M. (2000): Determinanten erwarteter Renditen am deutschen Aktienmarkt: Eine empirische Untersuchung anhand ausgewählter Kennzahlen, in: Zeitschrift für betriebswirtschaftliche Forschung, 2000, Vol. 52, p. 27-57

Weber, J. (2005): Das Advanced-Controlling-Handbuch: Alle entscheidenden Konzepte, Steuerungssysteme und Instrumente, in: Weber, J. (Ed.), Advanced Controlling, Weinheim 2005

Weber, J. (2008): Das Advanced-Controlling-Handbuch: Richtungsweisende Konzepte, Steuerungssysteme und Instrumente, in: Weber, J. (Ed.), Advanced Controlling, Vol. 2, Weinheim 2008

Weber, M. (2007): Genial einfach investieren: Mehr müssen Sie nicht wissen – das aber unbedingt !, Frankfurt am Main 2007

Wendt, R. (2009): Die Zufriedenheit mit Second Best Solutions von Konsumgütern in Abhängigkeit eines Ortswechsels, Series: Diplomarbeit, 2nd ed., Hamburg 2009

Werner C. (2009): Verbraucherbildung und Verbraucherberatung in der Altersvorsorge, Diss., Wiesbaden 2009

Wiedemann, P. (2010): Vorsorgeprinzip und Risikoängste: Zur Risikowahrnehmung des Mobilfunks, Wiesbaden 2010

Wiswede, G. (2007): Einführung in die Wirtschaftspsychologie, 4th ed., Munich 2007

Wunderle, S. (2006): Regret und Kundenloyalität: Eine kausalanalytische Untersuchung potentieller Ursachen interindividueller Unterschiede im Regret-Erleben und deren Auswirkungen im Konsumkontext, Diss., Wiesbaden 2006

Zajonz, R. (2010): Die Bewertung europäischer Immobilienaktien: Theoretische und empirische Modelle zur Erklärung der NAV-Spreads, in: Locarek-Junge, H., Röder, K., Wahrenburg, M. (Eds.), Finanzierung, Kapitalmarkt und Banken, Vol. 71, Diss., Lohmar – Cologne 2010

Zayer, E. (2007): Verspätete Projektabbrüche in F&E: Eine verhaltensorientierte Analyse, in: Weber, J. (Ed.), Schriften des Center for Controlling & Management (CCM), Vol. 25, Diss., Wiesbaden 2007

Ziegenbalg, B., Ziegenbalg, J. Ziegenbalg, O. (2007): Algorithmen: Von Hammurapi bis Gödel, 2nd ed., Frankfurt am Main 2007

Ziemba, W.T. (1991): Japanese security market regularities: Monthly, turn-of-the-month and year, holiday and golden week effects, in: Japan and the World Economy, 1991, Vol. 3, No. 2, p. 119-146

Zuzak, M.T. (2008): Ökonomische Analyse der Regulierung des Insiderhandels, in: Bernet, B., Geiger, H., Grünbichler, A., Hirszowicz, C., Kilgus, E., Spremann, K., Volkart, R. (Eds.), Bank- und finanzwirtschaftliche Forschungen, Vol. 387, Berne 2008

Internet sources:

Allianz Global Investors (2009): Portfolio Praxis: Akademie, Value oder Growth – mehr als eine Stilfrage. URL: http://docs.google.com/viewer?a=v&q=cache:6737Vafg6 l4J:www.allianzglobalinvestors.de/kapitalmarktanalyse/publikationen/PortfolioPraxis-Value-oder-Growth.pdf, dated on 08.02.2011.

Amel-Zadeh, A. (2008): The Return of the Size Anomaly: Evidence from the German Stock Market. URL: http://papers.ssrn.com/sol3/papers.cfm?abstract_id=952472, dated on 08.02.2011.

Arneth, S., Fleischer, J., Gerke, W. (1999): Kursgewinne bei Aufnahmen in den DAX 100, Verluste bei Entnahmen: Indexeffekt am deutschen Kapitalmarkt. URL: http://docs.google.com/viewer?a=v&q=cache:FuTxj2GJcGwJ:joergfleischer.com/Publi kationen/Indexeffekt.PDF, dated on 08.02.2011.

Barberis, N., Shleifer, A., Vishny, R. (n/a): "A model of investor sentiment". URL: http://docs.google.com/viewer?a=v&q=cache:W5eUVZua5toJ:badger.som.yale.edu/fac-ulty/ncb25/bsv_nonac.pdf, dated on 08.02.2011.

Bloed, P. (2008): Deutsche Aktien: Groß und günstig. URL: http://www.focus.de/finan-zen/boerse/aktien/deutsche-aktien-gross-und-guenstig_aid_300074.html, dated on 08.02 .2011.

Brosy, M. (2010): Börstenstrategien – Value-Growth-Strategie. URL: http://www.boer-senpoint.de/blog/borsenstrategien-value-growth-strategie/, dated on 08.02.2011.

Chen, G. (n/a): Short-run momentum and long-run reversals. URL: http://www.duke.e-du/~gwc/Behavioral%20explanations%20for%20short.htm, dated on 08.02.2011.

Csizi, V. (2010): Aktienmarkt: M- und S-DAX: Klein aber fein. URL: http://www.tag-esspiegel.de/wirtschaft/m-und-s-dax-klein-und-fein/1860836.html, dated on 08.02.2011.

Faulhaber, O. (2008): Spekulationsblasen: Modellierung mit Methoden der Hydrody-namik. URL: http://docs.google.com/viewer?a=v&q=cache:qIzmbSiI-s4J:www.oliverf-aulhaber.de/talks/Seminar_2008_FSS.pdf, dated on 08.02.2011.

FAZ (2001): Behavioral Finance: Substanzwerte schlagen Wachstumswerte. URL: http://www.faz.net/s/Rub4B891837ECD14082816D9E088A2D7CB4/Doc~E97563D32 E2E044489D3861D3981D7D5E~ATpl~Ecommon~Scontent.html,   dated   on 08.02.2011

FAZ (2002): Indizes: Ausländische Werte im S&P 500 werden ersetzt. URL: http://www.fazfinance.net/Aktuell/Boerse-und-Anlage/Auslaendische-Werte-im-SandP-500-werden-ersetzt-7929.html, dated on 08.02.2011.

FAZ (2004): Nebenwerte-Fonds: Indexfonds toppt fast alle gemanagten Produkte – und ist billiger. URL: http://www.fazfinance.net/Aktuell/Boerse-und-Anlage/Indexfonds-schlaegt-fast-alle-gemanagten-Produkte-und-ist-billiger-3966.html,   dated   on 08.02.2011.

FAZ (2004): Börsenzyklen: Der schlechteste Börsenmonat steht vor der Tür. URL: http://www.faz.net/-00n82w, dated on 08.02.2011.

Finanz-lexikon (2011): Wochenend-effekt. URL: http://www.finanz-lexikon.de/wochenend-effekt_3996.html, dated on 08.02.2011.

Finanztest (2011): Wochenendeffekt. URL: http://www.finanzentest.de/lexikon/1770/Wochenendeffekt.html, dated on 08.02.2011.

Fischbacher, U. (n/a): Psychology for finance. URL: http://docs.google.com/viewer?a= v&q=cache:-bh337rDmJIJ:www.iew.uzh.ch/study/courses/downloads/behfin04.pdf, dated on 08.02.2011.

Friedrich, C., Nitzsch, R. (n/a): Behavioral Finance: Erkenntnisse einer verhaltenswissenschaftlichen Kapitalmarktforschung. URL: http://docs.google.com/viewer?a=v&q= cache:2svPfNsVNcgJ:www.commendo.de/rw_e7v/commendo2/usr_documents/Nitzsch _Aufsatz_Behavioral-Finance.pdf, dated on 08.02.2011.

Damodaran, A. (n/a): Small Cap and Growth Investing. URL: http://docs.google.com/ viewer?a=v&q=cache:yUK5aerwYcgJ:www.stern.nyu.edu/~adamodar/pdfiles/invphiloh/gro wthN.pdf, dated on 08.02.2011.

Damodaran, A. (n/a): Graham's disciplines: Value Investing. URL: http://docs.google. com/viewer?a=v&q=cache:a6LmzK1i78sJ:www.stern.nyu.edu/~adamodar/pdfiles/invp hil/ch8.pdf, dated on 08.02.2011.

Dimitrov-Ludwig, P., Glebe, H., Hausdorf, J., Junge, N., Mattern, S., Sowka, E. (2003/2004): Zinsrisikomanagement und der Jahresabschluss von Kreditinstituten, Thema 7: Grenzen des Ansatzes aller Finanztitel zum Marktwert. URL: http://docs.google.com/viewer?a=v&q=cache:p5ZyTMkbqp8J:www1.uni-hamburg.de/ Kapitalmaerkte/download/SeminarWiSe200304Folien7.pdf, dated on 08.02.2011.

Google (n/a): Investor sentiment and the Closed-end fund puzzle. URL: http://docs.google.com/viewer?a=v&q=cache:cDH8B5SHdv8J:www.mtholyoke.edu/ac ad/econ/muturi.ppt, dated on 08.02.2011.

Hens, T. (2003): Behavioral and Evolutionary Finance. URL: http://docs.google.com/ viewer?a=v&q=cache:K34308SjPb0J:www.behavioralfinance.ch/domains/behavioralfi- nance_ch/data/Catalog/101008/ZuerichFinNeu.pdf, dated on 08.02.2011.

Höfling, M. (2010): SDAX und MDAX: Die zweite Börsenliga schlägt den DAX. URL: http://www.welt.de/finanzen/geldanlage/article11517991/Die-zweite-Börsenliga- schlaegt-den-Dax.html, dated on 08.02.2011.

IBC (n/a): Tulip timetable. URL: http://www.prod.bulbsonline.org/ibs/se/publiek/info- rmation.jsf/Information/flowerbulb-history/Tulip-time-table.html, dated on 08.02.2011.

Jaunich, A., Nitzsch, R. (2009): Verbreitung und Erfolg von Behavioral-Finance- Anlagestrategien in deutschen und amerikanischen Publikumsfonds. URL: http://docs.google.com/viewer?a=v&q=cache:j8GLqOv_WuUJ:www.efi.rwth-aachen. de/downloads/Forschung/WorkingPaper/workingpaper2009-01.pdf, dated on 08.02.2011.

Jungermann, H. (2007): Homo oeconomicus – unter der Lupe. URL: http://docs.goog- le.com/viewer?a=v&q=cache:lWfbFcdiEs0J:www.gp.tu-berlin.de/Users/j/jungermann/ Publications/WISU27.Equity_Premium.pdf, dated on 08.02.2011.

Kappeler, M. (2007): Das Closed-End Fund Puzzle am Beispiel von Schweizer Betei- ligungsgesellschaften. URL: http://docs.google.com/viewer?a=v&q=cache:b_kNxI969Y cJ:www.isb.uzh.ch/publikationen/pdf/publ_1355.pdf, dated on 08.02.2011.

Keimling, N. (2004): Einfache Value-Strategien zahlen sich aus: Das Kurs-Gewinn- Verhältnis. URL: http://docs.google.com/viewer?a=v&q=cache:3C1OGWbfFW4J:star- capital.de/files/KGV-Value-Strategie_Keimling.pdf, dated on 08.02.2011.

Keimling, N. (2005): Schwaches Wachstum zahlt sich aus: Das Kurs-Buchwert-Verhältnis. URL: http://docs.google.com/viewer?a=v&q=cache:geJ2RgSMd1sJ: www.antizyklisch-investieren.de/analysen/KBV-Value-Strategie_Keimling.pdf, dated on 08.02.2011.

Kohler, T. (2010): Der Beitrag der Behavioral-Finance-Theorie zur Erklärung von Finanzmarktanomalien. URL: http://issuu.com/seenplatte/docs/behavioral_finance_theorie, dated on 08.02.2011.

Kolahi, F. (2006): Turn-of-the month effect for the European stock market. URL: http://ir.lib.sfu.ca/handle/1892/3412, dated on 08.02.2011.

Küng, R. (2010): An welchem Kalenderatag soll ein Momentum portfolio rebalanciert werden ?. URL: http://webcache.googleusercontent.comwww.isb.uzh.ch/publikationen/ pdf/2747.pdf, dated on 08.02.2011.

Marmer, H.S. (2004): Why Small is Still Beautiful. URL: http://docs.google.com/ viewer?a=v&q=cache:w7xFfEWjjcEJ:www.ftinstitutional.ca/ca/inst/en/pdf/ commentary/whitepapers/white_paper_small_caps_081804.pdf, dated on 08.02.2011.

Maydorn, A. (2009): First Solar: Kurssprung nach Indexaufnahme. URL: http://www.deraktionaer.de/aktien-usa/first-solar--kurssprung-nach-indexaufnahme-10922479.htm, dated on 08.02.2011.

Merk, G. (n/a): Sell-in-May-Effect (Sell-in-May effect; sell in May and go away). URL: http://www.ad-hoc-news.de/sell-in-may-effekt--/de/Boersenlexikon/16332716, dated on 08.02.2011.

Nitzsch, R. (2007): Asset Management von Stiftungen, Welche Risiken gehören in den Einkaufskorg ?. URL: http://docs.google.com/viewer?a=v&q=cache:rcT5jfRk4J:www. suche.stiftungen.org/files/original/galerie_vom_12.02.2007_14.45.46/AssetManageme-nt_Lunchmeeting_HSH_Nordbank_Prof._Dr._Ruediger_von_Nitzsch.pdf, dated on 08.02.2011.

Ramsundhar, S. (1995): The turn of the month effect continued: A large comparison of small cap stocks and large cap stocks. URL: http://docs.google.com/viewer?a=v&q =cache:Kd5KpTxHmAUJ:ir.lib.sfu.ca/dspace/bitstream/1892/10976/1/GAWM%25202 008,%2520Ramsundhar,%2520S..pdf, dated on 08.02.2011.

Reiche, L. (2010): DAX Geflüster: Klein schlägt groß. URL: http://www.manager-magazin.de/finanzen/artikel/0,2828,711496-2,00.html, dated on 08.02.2011.

Rutz, M. (2009): Marktanomalien am Schweizer Aktienmarkt. URL: http://docs.google .com/viewer?a=v&q=cache:nveOPEhDWe4J:www.isb.uzh.ch/publikationen/pdf/publ_2 005.pdf, dated on 08.02.2011.

Salm, C., Siemkes, J. (n/a): Persistenz von Kalenderanomalien am deutschen Aktienmarkt. URL: http://docs.google.com/viewer?a=v&q=cache:xmOQ4NOQr_EJ:www.wiwiuni-muenster.de/me/downloads/Veroeffentlichungen/SalmSiemkes.pdf, dated on 08.02.2011.

Schwarz, H. (n/a): Erklärungsansätze der Behavioral Finance für Boom-Bust Sequenzen am Aktienmarkt. URL: http://docs.google.com/viewer?a=v&q= cache:3HiLHtTo0EwJ:finanzportal.wiwi.uni-saarland.de/behav/boom_bust.PDF, dated on 08.02.2011.

Shapiro, D. (n/a): Cross-section of Average Returns. URL: http://docs.google.com/ viewer?a=v&q=cache:52eIIfa7NHoJ:www.belkcollege.uncc.edu/dashapir/SeminarPhDClass 8.pdf, dated on 08.02.2011.

SmartInMoney (2010): Stock Market Anomaly – January Effect. URL: http://smartinmoney.com/january_effect.aspx, dated on 08.02.2011.

Spaulding, W.C. (2005-2011): Market Anomalies. URL: http://thismatter.com/money/ investments/market-anomalies.htm, dated on 08.02.2011.

Standard & Poor's (2008): The Shrinking Index Effect: A Global Perspective. URL: http://docs.google.com/viewer?a=v&q=cache:gLiWWmB7f30J:www2.standardandpoor s.com/spf/pdf/index/The_Shrinking_Index_Effect.pdf, dated on 08.02.2011.

Web Lexikon (2004): Spekulationsblase. URL: http://www.zzzzz.de/lexikon/s/sp/ spekulationsblase.html, dated on 08.02.2011.